MOVING BEYOND COMPROMISE

Why Stop There?

Kevin C. Smith
Michael T. Burke
Gordon P. McComb

Moving Beyond Compromise: *Why Stop There?*

DEDICATION

This book is dedicated to anyone who has been through the difficult process of making decisions in the context of a business setting or for that matter any setting in which several people need to agree on a course of action. To characterize this process as frustrating is to minimize the feelings we have all had many times when attempting to reach agreement on even trivial issues. Our hope is that the ideas and processes presented here will help others understand that decision-making does not have to be a painful experience.

CONTENTS

ACKNOWLEDGMENTS

The process of writing a book may seem to be solitary, even though several authors may be collaborating, but in reality it affects and involves many others. Family and friends are ignored and then drafted into reading the work, with the hoped-for result of a positive review and useful suggestions for improvements.

We want to give our heartfelt thanks to our wives, Juli Redson-Smith, Susan Bowling, and Lauren McComb. They have put up with the multiyear process of creating this book with cheerful support and willingness to see us meet and spend the time we needed to write and then rewrite it and also their reading and commenting on various drafts. In fact, we owe the title to Lauren and thank her for that service.

We also want to thank our children, Gwen Kramer, Cheresse Burke, and Lindsay McComb and her husband, David Precht, for reviewing and then commenting extensively about it. They are all busy with family and work, and their time has been an invaluable gift to us.

We also want to thank our hardworking editor, Cindy Opong. We also had a number of friends and colleagues who were willing to review and comment, including Larry Jones, Doug Allen, Phil Shires, Michele Mortensen, and Jennifer Trembley.

We are deeply indebted to them for their ideas and help.

How do three very different personalities manage to work together over a period of years, creating and discarding various ideas, premises, drafts, and story lines, and still remain on speaking terms at the end of the process? In our case, the answer is simple: we actually practice the very rules that we advocate here, which are based on the principle of consultation used in decision-making within the Bahá'í Faith, of which the authors are members. The Bahá'í approach has been used successfully by millions of its members for more than a century and a half and has proven to be effective in a variety of local, regional, national, and international settings and situations. While the Bahá'í Faith does not have a written set of rules as set forth here, the basic structure of our rules does conform with the principle of consultation.

This book is not an attempt to "sell" the Bahá'í Faith or any aspect of it. Our purpose here is simply to present an approach to decision-making and problem solving that can result in workable solutions - hence, the process name Solution-Building is used to provide a term that summarizes our intent. We believe that any group decision, whether in business, family, charitable organizations, politics, or any other setting, can benefit from these principles.

INTRODUCTION

The process of making decisions is integral to life. We make decisions every day, from what to have for breakfast to critical issues of life and business. When two or more people are involved in making those decisions, the process often involves "compromise" and can be complicated by the basic give-and-take and trade-offs that are associated with this approach.

Webster's New Twentieth Century Dictionary of the English Language defines compromise in this way:

- A settlement in which each side gives up some demands or makes concessions

- An adjustment of opposing principles, systems, etc., in which part of each is given up

- The result of such an adjustment or settlement

- Something midway between different things

- A laying open to danger, suspicion, or disrepute, as a *compromise* of one's good name, or; to surrender or give up (one's interest, principles, etc.)

Compromise necessarily, then, leads to a result that has the great risk of being suboptimal because the concessions made can easily preclude consideration of alternatives and important viewpoints. One of the factors that those who promote compromise as a means of making decisions use as justification is that each side gives up something they want, and thus each side can "live with" the result. In reality, neither side will give up something critically important to them while expecting the other to do just that. The end result is often that either no decision or agreement can be reached or one or both of the parties is unhappy with the result. Too frequently, the ultimate result is failure because one or both parties do not fully support the agreement, which becomes more likely if one party feels it gave more than the other or had to give up something related to its principles or best interest.

In an increasingly complex world, compromise is not the best way to reach decisions. An approach that fully and objectively examines all points of view and ideas is needed to arrive at workable solutions to problems and issues as diverse as those we see in the world today.

Anyone who has worked inside any company, large or small, knows that it is often very challenging to make decisions. Different personalities, diverse interactions, company politics, and even social, political, and economic philosophies present barriers to agreement. Add to that the basic competitive nature of human beings and the result can be a bubbling stewpot of rancor, foxhole-digging, foot-dragging, backbiting, criticism, individual conflict, and an attitude of an "I win, you lose" zero-sum game that leads to, at best, nonoptimal decisions and at worst, paralysis and no decisions at all.

This description applies to virtually any type of organization, not just the corporate setting. It can be seen in organizations, nonprofits, politics, families, churches, schools, and any other setting in which a group of people, whether it be two or many, must meet and make decisions on any topic. All of us have seen the results of committee deliberations aimed at making decisions in a number of these seemingly different settings. Quite often, when we watch the process, we understand the saying that "A committee is a cul-de-sac down which ideas are lured and then quietly strangled." The three authors have worked in a variety of different companies and noncorporate settings, including small local companies (fewer than 10 employees) to very large multinational corporations; they have been a part of boards of directors and trustees of nonprofits, school and church groups, neighborhood organizations, and others. They have all had the (mis)fortune of serving on committees charged with making decisions ranging from purchasing equipment to basic corporate strategy for international product development. Some of these committees have been effective, but most have not achieved the combined potential of their members. In many cases, trouble began when one or more of the members let their personal agendas interfere with any sort of group discussion and consensus. Too often this was accompanied by clashes between individuals, mutual criticism, arguments, and backbiting. When decisions were finally reached and recommendations and plans prepared, part of the group undermined the decision by making it clear to those outside the committee that they did not support the results. This common behavior was often successful in sabotaging the work of the committee.

In other cases, the committee or group was dominated by a single individual with strongly expressed opinions and ideas. This person was generally the most senior member of the group, was accustomed to making the decisions, and expected them to simply be accepted. To this person, the group was just a rubber stamp validating his will.

In all of these cases, the probability of an effective decision being reached and then any associated plans or recommendations acted on with enthusiasm and dedication is not nearly as high as it should be. Human nature, for most of us, includes a desire to not only do a good job on any task we are given but also to have that effort respected and recognized. When we spend time in meetings arriving at decisions and making plans or recommendations only to see them either torpedoed, ignored, or poorly acted upon, we naturally feel, at the very least, disappointed and with continued rejections, we often become depressed and withdraw from participating.

We believe there is a better way, a way in which all participants will feel a part of the group and will then take a full role in it.

This better way is a process called "Solution-Building," which occurs when a group of individuals meets and agrees to a few simple rules to follow in their deliberations. The quality of the result will rise, and then the implementation will be more enthusiastically embraced. Our experience suggests that this will have a measurably positive influence on the company's bottom line and employee satisfaction, itself a factor that influences bottom-line performance.

Those few simple rules, which we call the "Guiding Principles," are the subject of this volume. Rather than just presenting a list, we have chosen to illustrate them in the form of a fictional company that desperately needs to make decisions that will determine the survival of the organization and by implication the livelihood of the employees who are called upon to make and then implement those decisions. As you read this story, you will not only learn these Guiding Principles but will also meet some characters and personalities who will help introduce them and whom you have most likely met during your careers.

A few words about political correctness in this book:

Please do not take any of these characters as being representative of a professional group as a whole. All professions have a full range of personality types and temperaments among their membership.

For consistency's sake, we refer to individuals generically as "he" and mean no slight to women thereby. Obviously, where gender is implied or specified, by name or some other means, the proper pronouns and other parts of speech are used.

So now, the story of JayOGrafix, Lilly O'Hara, and the need to survive.

CAST OF CHARACTERS
(in order of appearance)

Lilly O'Hara	Owner and CEO of JayOGrafix
Steve Parsons	"Time Traveler"
Mark McCoy	VP, HR
Jim Cavanaugh	Production Director
Allison Thorpe	VP, Sales
Jason Halloran	VP, R&D
Pat	Assistant to Lilly
Kelly Hong	Section Head, R&D
Bob Hernandez	R&D Associate Director
Mara Parsons	Steve's wife
Ken Fujita	VP, Engineering
Stan Hadley	CIO
J. Bradley LaSalle	VP and General Counsel
Donna Lewis	CFO
Bill Matthews	Marketing Director

CHAPTER ONE

Lilly O'Hara walked at a pace that allowed her to think about the morning. It had not gone well.

She had arrived at the company early to prepare for today's senior management meeting. As she sat down at her desk, the phone started ringing, which led to the first of a round of frustrating sessions with people who wanted their way and only their way and were willing to be loud, rude, caustic, sarcastic, profane, aggressively contentious, and uncompromising to get it. Then, at the senior management meeting later that morning, behavior was worse than it had been for months.

The company, JayOGrafix, called JOG by customers and employees alike, was in serious trouble. Sales of their high-end video graphics equipment and related products had been falling for a year and recently had fallen even faster partially because their major competitor, Haze Systems, was rumored to have a new and very advanced product nearly ready for the market, and potential customers were waiting to see it. Another factor, though, was that the founder of the company, JJ O'Hara, had died a few months ago. He had been the source of most of the company's advances and a charismatic leader who had held together a diverse group of highly intelligent and competitive scientists and engineers for years. His loss had been a blow to employee morale, and they had been struggling since his death. This included the senior management team.

Today's meeting was to have concentrated on how to get the company out of the financial hole it found itself in with the death of JJ. Lilly, his only child and heir, suddenly found that she owned the company, which she had joined several years before after earning an advanced degree in electrical engineering. She had also become COO two months before JJ died, which caused resentment on the part of many, and had not led to ready acceptance of her leadership by other senior, long-time staff. They constantly challenged her. Sometimes, she just wanted to fire the entire bunch or at least some of them. She recognized, though, that there was no time to find or train a new team with the necessary knowledge and skills.

When you have several people in a room who only want their way, she thought, *nothing happens. And when nothing happens, the company fails. Why can't they see that? Why won't they listen to each other? Why won't they look for the good points of other people's ideas instead of launching personal attacks? They're big in the brains department, but their egos seem ten times as big! I wonder how Dad stood for it and how I can get them to sit down at the table without fighting and holding to their own agendas. I don't know how much longer we can last. How can I get them to look at the good things we are doing and focus on our future?*

These and other questions were on her mind as she arrived at The Corner Deli, a small place a couple of blocks from the company where she thought she would get a sandwich and a cup of coffee and calm down. No one from the company ever came here for lunch, as they preferred a fancier place that lay in the opposite direction. Here, she was hoping to have some time alone to think.

The Corner Deli looked like something from another era: glass coolers of drinks, sandwich fixings and sides, an antique wooden cash register, fans in the ceiling, wooden counters, tables, and chairs. After ordering her lunch and telling the young woman behind the counter that she wanted to eat in, Lilly looked around in wonder, thinking she had never seen anything like this place. Then she realized that even though it had a feeling of spaciousness there were only nine tables of varying sizes, and all were full of people enjoying their lunches. *Oh*, she thought as she picked up her lunch, *the table back in the far corner is available.* She started toward it but noticed that it was not empty; a man was sitting at one end. He was well dressed and looked to be in his mid-sixties. She hesitated and then decided she could sit at the other end.

She approached the table but paused for a moment before setting her lunch down. She asked, "Do you mind if I sit at this end?"

"Not at all. I was planning to leave shortly, so please sit any-where you like," he said with a friendly smile. Lilly noticed that he had what her father called "smile wrinkles" around his eyes, which were a bright, alert blue. She then noticed he was wearing a neatly pressed suit and thought he looked quite distinguished. "Thank you, sir." She sat.

And sat, staring at her sandwich and cup of coffee. The events of the morning came back to her in a rush, and she suddenly went from feeling hungry to having no appetite at all. Lilly shoved the plate into the middle of the table disgustedly and was ready to leave. For the first time since her father died, she felt ready to cry, not from grief but frustration. She stared at the middle of the table thinking she could not give up but had no idea what to do.

"Excuse me, I don't mean to intrude, but you seem quite troubled." It was the man at the end of the table. The look of concern on his face was so genuine that she suddenly felt this strange urge to unburden herself to him.

"Uh, I'm having a tough time at work and am wondering what to do about it. That's all."

"Would you like to talk about it?"

"I thought you were leaving."

"I'm not in a hurry. I don't meet my wife for another hour or so." He smiled, and Lilly thought perhaps if she just talked about it she might come up with some ideas that would help.

"By the way, I'm Steve, Steve Parsons," he said, standing and extending a hand.

"I'm Lilly O'Hara," she said, taking his hand in a firm grip. He took a seat in a chair closer to Lilly.

Then she told him her story. He looked very sympathetic as she talked about her father and his death and what effect it had on her and on the company.

When she told him about the behavior of her staff at several meetings over the past few weeks and especially this morning's session, he said, "Yes, I can see that's quite frustrating. This has been going on for weeks? They behave the same at each meeting? No one actually moves off their position?"

"Yes. Yes. And yes. Every meeting is like entering a time warp. We seem to go back to the same place each and every time."

"Do you think they really care for the future of the company?"

"Actually, I do. Most of them were with Dad from the beginning, and I have known some of them since I was in grade school. Maybe that's part of the reason I can't get them to work together; they don't take me seriously. Maybe I need to fire these guys and work with someone new. Each of them thinks that only they have the answer to our problems, and they're not willing to even look at anything else. I didn't realize there was so much competition between them or that it could be so destructive. I have seen people I always thought were friends at each other's throats over this. Some of them can barely talk with each other anymore."

"Maybe you do need to fire some of them," said Steve, "and maybe not, but you already said you don't have time to get someone in who will work well with you and all the others. Perhaps you need to find a way to get them to work as a team."

"I just don't know what to do to get them to work together. They spend all their time poking holes in each other's ideas to the point that it is impossible to critically and objectively evaluate any of them."

"What if I told you there is a way? If they really want to solve the problem, there's a collaborative approach to true consultation called Solution-Building. That, if your group will use it, will focus them entirely on coming up with the best solution to the problem. It can be used, actually, to solve any problem or issue."

"Them? Are you from another planet? This crew has a problem even being civil to each other around the water cooler."

"Has it always been that way? Was there ever a time when they got along and worked together?"

"Well, yes, they used to be a team, but now ... I don't know, maybe they're just overstressed with all the problems we are having. Actually, they did clash a lot, but Dad kept them in line. He had a strong personality and presence."

"Then," Steve said with a smile, "they can do it again, but they need a new framework for working and making decisions that's different from what they have been using. One that is based on mutual respect, civility, openness to new ideas, a willingness to listen and learn, and, most of all, taking their egos out of the equation."

"And you have something?" Her tone sounded skeptical.

"Possibly, but it requires a group of people willing to use that framework."

"Now I know you are from another planet. Even before Dad died, they did not behave that way."

"Not from another planet, just a different way of looking at things. A way that things will be done in the future."

"So you are a time traveler?"

"Maybe a future thinker," Steve said with a wide smile. "Do you want to hear about this consultation approach?"

Lilly hesitated, thinking this was crazy. Then she realized that she had no other ideas, so maybe this "time traveler" could spark something useful. "Does anyone use this 'consultation' or 'Solution-Building' approach, as you call it?"

"A few people do, and, when used properly, the results are actually quite amazing."

"Okay," she said, smiling for the first time since the day began, "please tell me about it. I'll try to be open and willing to hear. How do we even start?"

"Good question, and oh, by the way, being open and willing to learn is the first step. Why don't you tell me what a typical meeting is like. Who attends, what they say, how they interact with each other, and how you deal with it."

Lilly thought that morning's meeting was a good place to start. After all, it seemed to have been just like every other meeting she had been in for the past several weeks.

"Our senior management meeting includes the heads of R&D, engineering, production, marketing, HR, finance, legal, sales, and IT, along with me. Meetings normally start off with everyone being polite to each other in that tense way people will act when they are expecting things to get unpleasant. It always does, generally within the first five minutes. Most of the time it is the marketing guy who complains about production, the R&D guy is unhappy with his budget, or the CFO harps about increasing costs, lack of revenue, or money wasted. It has been so bad sometimes that I have ended the meetings early and literally ordered everyone from the room. People simply will not listen to each other, and each person seems to have their own agenda to push. On top of that, there is a lot of posturing, rancorous insults, dismissing of each other's ideas without consideration of any merits, and trying to verbally bully each other into agreement with them and them only. The egos just seem to clash rather than work together. I don't think we have had a productive meeting since Dad got really sick."

"Are there particular individuals who are more likely to engage in that behavior than others?"

"R&D, marketing, and finance are the main ones, but production and sales will get into it sometimes, as will legal. The only ones who mostly stay out of it are the heads of engineering, HR, and IT. They have their own ideas but are quieter than the others. In some ways, they are just as convinced they have the answers and will sometimes roadblock things too."

Steve thought for a few seconds, then took out a pen, looked around, and pulled an unused napkin to him. As he wrote, he said, "It sounds to me like you have nine people in the room besides yourself who are playing only by their own rules. That is why the first rule of Solution-Building is:

RULE 1: Everyone plays by the same rules.

"You see, unless everyone is abiding by the same principles, they will never even agree to what the problem is, much less be willing to use any sort of rational approach to evaluating ideas and reaching a solution." Then he added, "Lilly, do you play any sports?"

Lilly was taken aback by the seemingly abrupt change in subject. "Well, I was on the softball team when I was an undergrad, and I play tennis on weekends now. Why do you ask?"

Steve seemed to ignore the question and went on. "Softball is a good example. What would happen if one of the players on your team decided she should get four strikes instead of three, another that he should be allowed to walk after three balls, another that if he led off second base he could not be thrown out, or any other variation? If all the players played by different rules, rules that applied only to them, you could not play a game, any game, could you? It is the same in any sort of group activity and especially so when reaching important decisions in business or any other setting."

"I see how that could be problematic in softball, but how do I get my team to even think about that? You are right. They are each using their own set of rules, rules that are just different enough to make things difficult for everyone else. I just don't have a clue how to approach it and even get one of them to consider anything else, much less the entire crew."

"Yes, that may not be easy. I can toss a couple of ideas at you, and you can perhaps come up with others. One may be to call a meeting and not allow anyone to speak until you spell out the problem of different rules and agendas and then help the group understand the destructive nature of their current actions. That may or may not work with this group, but if it does, it saves time. Another idea could be to meet with each person alone and do the same thing. The advantage of this is that no one else is in the room to clash with, and they may be willing to listen. This is more time consuming but may be more successful. I am sure you can think of some other ideas as well."

Lilly thought a moment, and then a memory came back to her from years ago. "I had a political science class as an undergrad where we were divided into two groups to debate a subject that was then current. It got quite heated, and some of the participants said some pretty unpleasant things. At the beginning of the next class, after some of us hadn't spoken to each other for several days, the professor divided the class into the two groups again but informed us that we were to take the opposite stance and made it worth a significant portion of our grade if we did this seriously. I wonder if something like that would work."

"See, you are already getting good ideas!" Steve paused for a few seconds and then said, "Lilly, I can't emphasize too much the importance of this first rule. It is really all about justice." Seeing the puzzled look on Lilly's face, he quickly went on. "Let me explain what I mean. I'm not talking about legal systems or TV police shows. I'm talking about the individual sense of justice that a person carries around inside, that sense of fairness, of equity and impartiality that allows a person to view problems and solutions—with a mind that's clear and freed from the distractions of self-interest. Do you understand what I'm saying?"

"I think so, but I'm not sure I've met a lot of people capable of being that fair-minded."

"Sure you have, Lilly. Let's go back to our softball analogy, if you'll humor me for a moment."

"Be my guest. I'm all ears."

Steve stroked his mustache a couple of times in a gesture Lilly had noticed him make before. He seemed to do this whenever he was carefully considering his words. His eyes also wandered off into the distance momentarily before refocusing on hers. "Sometimes in baseball a player, even a very good hitter, may be called upon to lay down a bunt. If memory serves, this is called a *sacrifice*. And even though every instinct may be telling that player to swing away, he is willing, for a higher purpose, to do this. Why?"

"You're asking me? OK, well, maybe because his manager gave him the bunt sign?"

"Yes, but what else? Could it be that it's simply the correct move to make, the play with the best possible chance of a favorable outcome? It's late in the game, and your team is down a run. There's nobody out and a runner on first. What do you do?"

"You try to advance the runner into scoring position. OK, I get it, but so what?"

Steve shook his head with just a hint of a smile on his face. "It's the same situation you're in: late in the game and your team is down a run. You need people, fair-minded people, who are willing to step up to the plate and do what's right for the team. People who aren't going to swing for the fences just because it will make them look good. People capable of sacrificing their own self-interests in pursuit of something greater. People capable of impartially assessing a situation and wholeheartedly supporting a sound decision. And when you have such a team, they will truly all be playing by the same rules. Think about it."

Steve darted a quick glance at his watch. "Oops, I need to meet my wife."

"Wait. You mean to tell me you are leaving? But this approach of yours, this Solution-Building approach surely it can't be just 'Everyone plays by the same rules.' There is more, isn't there? Can't we talk more?"

Steve looked at her. "Yes there is much more, but I don't have time now. My wife and I have lunch here every Tuesday. If you really want to learn more, why don't you join us next week? We usually get here at about 12:30. Then you can tell us what success you have had."

I don't have time Tuesday, Lilly thought, *but this is helping*. "Okay, Steve, I will see you next week. Does your wife know about this idea as well?"

"Oh yes. She uses it a quite often and is better at it than I am. Here is how to contact me if you need to. See you then." He handed Lilly his business card and then turned and walked toward the front of the deli and out the door.

She looked at the card and saw:

Steve Parsons

Consultant

and a phone number.

Lilly sat staring at the door where her "time traveler" had just left, wondering who this person was, and what this method was he was talking about. She was feeling confused but strangely excited about learning more. She really wanted the company to do well and survive and felt that this approach might be something worth a try. She had always believed that things happen for a reason. Why did she come to this deli today, at this time? Why were there no other seats available, and why was Steve there?

What he had said made sense to her, but she did not see how just getting people to "play by the same rules" would do any good. What were the rules? How did you go about getting this dysfunctional group of egotists to agree to "rules" that were not their own? *I need an ally,* she realized, *someone who will both agree and work with me. But first, maybe I should do a bit of searching. What did Steve call it? Consultation, or was it collaborative Solution-Building? Maybe there is some information on the Internet I can use to see if this is in any way real or if he is just spinning fantasy.*

Then Lilly walked out the door, with her mostly uneaten lunch in hand, feeling that she wanted to find out if anything she just heard could help. She also found herself wondering if she should meet Steve and his wife on Tuesday to see if they had more to say that was useful. She was not certain she should spend her time with them at all but told herself to keep an open mind. She walked briskly back to the office.

CHAPTER TWO

On the way back, Lilly thought of the members of her executive team and asked herself if any of them would be likely to help her. She thought about those who were constantly at each other's throats and those who seemed to stay more or less on the sidelines during the more rancorous exchanges. *The most likely*, she thought, *would be Mark.* Mark McCoy was the HR director and seemed to be pretty open-minded, often saying in meetings that they needed to stop squabbling and make some decisions to help the company survive.

When she got to her desk, Lilly put in a call to Mark, leaving a message asking him to come over when he received it, and then turned to her computer. She started searching for information about consultation and Solution-Building.

Half an hour later, when Mark knocked on the doorframe, she had several pieces of information that made her feel more hopeful that this approach might help. That is, if she could get this crew to listen and respond.

"Hi, Lilly, I was looking for you about an hour ago to see if you wanted to get some lunch." Mark was no-nonsense and straightforward in his manner. Lilly liked that; it appealed to her engineering mind-set.

"Hi, Mark, please sit down. I want to bounce a couple of things off you."

She told Mark that she was frustrated with their team and was looking for a way to get them to work together. She briefly described what Steve had said to her without mentioning where she got the information, asking, "Have you ever heard about anything like this?"

"It sounds a bit like the brainstorming approach that many business consultants use. That's been around for decades. I've seen it work, and I've seen it fail."

"I know, but in this approach there is something about 'taking ego out' as a part of it, which I have never seen in any brainstorming session. Even in those sessions, people cling to their ideas, and their egos get in the way a lot of the time. Their own personal agendas seem more important than a successful outcome."

"Hmm, yes, that has always been an issue," said Mark. "As you saw on at least a few occasions, JJ had to beat them up verbally once in a while to get their attention. As a result, his ideas usually were the ones adopted, even if several of us thought there were other good ones to consider. Now that he is gone, they are feeling freer to push their own agendas. Seems to me they may have gone too far in that direction since they no longer listen to anyone else."

"Ah, yes, 'beat them up' as a means to get them to listen, but then Dad was the one that prevailed." *I wonder*, Lilly thought, *if that was a good thing.* She then realized she may have to find a way to do just that.

Mark was looking thoughtful. "I may have run across something like this before, but I can't clearly remember. At the time, I thought it was a pie-in-the-sky thing, but I will have to search for some information."

"Actually," said Lilly, "I did a little searching while I was waiting for you to come by and have found a couple of things. Take a look at this." Mark looked at the JOGpad that Lilly handed him, studied it for a few minutes, and clicked some of the page links.

After about five minutes, he said, "Looks intriguing to me, but I am not sure how we go about getting this crew to consider any of it."

"That's why I am glad you are here. I may have to take some drastic action, and I need your support and help." She and Mark discussed some ideas for the next hour. They then outlined a plan to figuratively "beat them up" and exert Lilly's authority to get their participation.

The next morning Lilly arrived at her usual early hour, noting that she was not the only one in already. She saw Mark's car in the lot as well as a few others. She went straight to her desk and, ignoring the blinking message light on her phone, called Mark and asked him to come over as soon as he could. Then she sat and thought for a few minutes. She needed to make sure Mark was ready for what she knew she would have to do later that day. For that matter, she needed to make sure she, herself, was ready.

"Mark, who do you think is going to be my biggest problem today?"

Mark replied slowly, "Well, I think we both know who the problems will be. They all think they are the sole reason the company is surviving at all, and that they are the only ones who can keep us alive."

"Do you think any of them are justified?"

"Frankly, no. No one person or department is capable of doing that. In my opinion, the contempt they have for everyone else is part of what's killing us."

"Mark, if worst comes to worst and any one of these three decides to leave the company, I will need to know who can take their place. In your opinion, who can replace each of them with the least disruption? I don't mean the nominal second in command, but who can best do the job?"

"Give me some time to think about it, and I will get back to you later this afternoon."

———◦≈≈≈◦———

Lilly was in her office until 11:00, when the Friday morning weekly meeting was to start—another executive meeting that usually was contentious and often completely unproductive. *A good forum for what I think I have to do*, she thought as she walked to the conference room.

Mark joined her on the way. "Make your decision yet?"

"I'm keeping an open mind, but I think I know what will happen." Mark, realizing that was all he would get, did not respond.

Entering the conference room, Lilly noted that the directors of R&D, finance, and marketing were not there. These three were her biggest problems and always seemed to vie for being the last to arrive. Lilly decided to start the meeting on time with or without them.

"OK, let's get started," she said, looking at the production director. "Jim, how did the week go?" All the others, the directors of engineering, IT, legal affairs, sales, and advertising, looked at each other and Lilly in confusion. This was not the way things usually started; Lilly had always waited for The Triplets, as they were known, to arrive.

"Uh, well, we met our production numbers for the week, and there were no major glitches or problems. Of course, with the unit sales down, meeting the numbers wasn't very difficult."

"Thanks, Jim. Allison, how about our sales figures? How was the week, and what are the trends?"

Again, looks went around the table. Without The Triplets, the production summary was not challenged, sneered at, or attacked. Also, Lilly seemed to be much more direct, more tense, and angrier than she had ever been in one of these meetings.

Allison looked nervous and unhappy. "They are down about two percent this week, which is better than the trends, which are more like three to four. We did get our annual order from Trigeminus, which is why we weren't down more. I think we can't expect the trends to change significantly from the past several months. In fact, from what my staff is hearing from our contacts, we can expect further erosion of sales while the market waits for the new Haze Systems product to come out. We are hearing some premarket hype, and I would sure like to know what R&D thinks about it."

"Thanks, Allison. I appreciate the honesty, and I would like to hear from R&D on that too. I would like you to start forwarding the dailies to me as well. I want to stay on top of it from now on." She looked around, obviously annoyed that three directors were missing and were already ten minutes late. "Mark, anything from HR?"

"Not much. I am getting a lot of questions about how soon we are going to start laying people off. I have, so far, been able to assure people that we have no plans to do that, but after hearing Allison's report, I wonder if we need a furlough plan or even a plan to reduce staff. The major question will be where we can, or maybe should, make those cuts."

"Not in R&D," said Jason Halloran, the R&D director who was standing in the doorway, the last of The Triplets to enter the room. "There is no one we can do without. If we are going to have a competitive product, we should actually expand our staff." He remained standing in the door while the directors of finance and marketing found places at the table, then strode into the room, and sat at the far end of the table from Lilly. All three were scowling. There were mutterings of complaint about the meeting starting without them.

"If you don't want the meeting to start without you," said Lilly, "be here on time. We will not repeat anything for the benefit of people who can't show up when the meeting is scheduled." She looked at each in turn, the R&D director last. All three glared at her angrily.

"I have important things to do," said Jason, "and I don't consider meetings to be at the top of the list. Nothing important ever happens here anyway." The other two Triplets nodded in assent. *No*, thought Lilly, *you three won't allow it.*

"Jason, I don't see anyone in the room who doesn't have important things to do, including me. And I consider this meeting, and any of the meetings of this group, to be important enough to devote my time to. I expect all of you to do the same. Am I clear?" Lilly spoke in a clear, calm voice and kept her expression neutral.

The room was silent. Jason just sat and glared at Lilly and finally gave a curt nod.

"Now," said Lilly, "for a few changes." She looked around at faces showing curiosity, fear and, again, anger.

"What changes?" asked Jason.

"We are going to have some rules to follow in our meetings. I plan to introduce the first one today." Again, she looked around, but before she could go on, Jason said in a harsh voice, "Rules? What rules? We don't need rules for meetings. They already exist. They're called Robert's Rules of Order. Why do YOU think we …"

"That's enough," Lilly said loudly and firmly. "you will keep quiet while I continue. I am still the CEO, and for once you will pipe down and listen. Clear?" There were a couple of gasps, and Jason again glared at Lilly but did not say a word. "I asked if that was clear, Jason."

After a few seconds, Jason simply said, "Yes." His tone of voice implied the opposite.

Lilly reached down to her JOGpad and touched a key. The JOGboard behind her came to life, and the group saw:

RULE 1: Everyone plays by the same rules.

A few seconds of silence was followed by, "What kind of rule is that? What does it mean? We already play by the same rules!" Several people agreed, and Lilly noted the loudest were the directors of finance and marketing and Jason. "This is a waste of time when we could be doing something useful. Where did this come from anyway?" The meeting was beginning to turn chaotic, so Lilly used a trick she learned from a college professor.

"Really, Jason?" she said in a soft voice. The room became very quiet. "And which of the same rules do you play by? The one that says you are on time for our meetings? And we have already discussed the importance of these meetings." Jason turned bright red and opened his mouth to speak again.

But Lilly went on before he could start. "No one in this group seems to understand the importance of this concept. That's because unless we are all on the same track, page, or whatever you want to call it, we will never accomplish anything because you people spend your time bickering and blaming each other. We have a companywide problem: survival. Unless we are all working together, we will not be in business much longer. The only way we can work together is to play by the same consistent rules."

There were a number of snorts from the people around the table. So many that Lilly was not certain who had made the sounds. Jason spoke loudly and angrily.

"The first rule ought to be not to waste any more time on this kind of nonsense and get on with the meeting. I don't know how you came up with this, and I don't care. I want to hear what production and sales had to say before I got here and then get on with the meeting and back to my work." Again, some at the table were talking and agreeing with Jason, while others were quietly listening. A few were nodding their heads, but Lilly was not sure if they were agreeing with Jason or her.

Lilly decided to keep going. "This is merely the first of several rules we will discuss beginning with Tuesday's meeting. We are going to change the way we make decisions by using a process called Solution-Building, an approach that just may help us to survive as a company. I have been studying this approach, and there are a number of other rules, including not criticizing other people's ideas or suggestions." The reaction was immediate and to Lilly's great surprise, quite negative.

"Solution-Building, what the heck is that?"

"Waste of time. Just make a decision, and tell us what to do!"

"As if these meetings weren't bad enough, turn them into a debating club and we will never get anything done. Where have you been studying this stuff? Some whoo-whoo Internet site? Is this some New Age feel-good claptrap?"

And more, none of it positive. Lilly noted that some of the participants had kept quiet, but nearly everyone looked confused, annoyed or outright angry. The loudest of the complaints came from The Triplets. Then she got angry. She was going to have to do something before things got completely out of control. She stood up and slapped her pad of paper on the table. "Enough!" Silence followed, and again Jason opened his mouth. "Don't say a word," she said in a commanding tone none of them had ever heard her use. He closed his mouth, a startled expression on his face. Several others started to speak, but seeing the expression on her face, chose not to.

"How many of you want this company to survive and prosper? How many? I want a show of hands. Now!" Mark and Allison raised their hands immediately, as did the directors of engineering, IT, and advertising. Slowly, the production director raised his, as did the legal director. Two of The Triplets sat with their hands lowered for a few seconds and then gradually raised them. Jason looked angrily at the others and then raised his.

Lilly found her anger rising rapidly and tried to suppress it, with limited success. "I see that some of you are not certain you even want this company to survive. I am going to give you a little homework assignment, and we will continue this meeting on Tuesday at 10 a.m. Your assignment is to spend the weekend asking yourselves if you even want a job at all. Think about whether or not you want to play by the same rules. And consider this: if you do not want to do that, as well as other rules I will give you, you will not have a job very much longer because either I will fire you or this company will fold, and there will be no jobs to have."

She turned, walked out of the room, and went to her office, telling her assistant, Pat, she did not want to be disturbed. She stood looking out her window for a long time, trying to calm down after the contentious meeting. She did not believe she was the type of manager that would just fire someone on the spot without some type of understanding. She also knew deep down that if she did not do something, and quickly, JOG would be in the history books soon. Lilly knew Jason was a long-term employee who had contributed a great deal to the success of the company. After several long minutes, she decided she needed to speak with Jason directly and privately. Lilly decided it would be best to call him immediately. Jason answered on the first ring and agreed to meet. He said he would be in her office right away.

Still standing, Lilly greeted Jason as he entered the room. She could tell by his appearance that he wanted this meeting, and that he probably had been stewing about this ever since the staff meeting abruptly ended. "Lilly," Jason said, "this company has been around a long time and has been very successful without silly ideas, magazine articles, Internet searches, and, frankly, even without you. Your father put a great team together, and we built this company into what it is. Why do you want to tear all that apart?"

Lilly was surprised at this immediate outburst. She had hoped by this discussion to get Jason on her side, but clearly this was not to be. "My father did build a great team and company, but we are way down in sales, our technology is behind our competitors, some of our best people have left, and we are seriously at risk of failure. Do you read any of the weekly reports? Do you pay attention in any of the meetings? Do you follow at all what our competition is doing? The market does not move slowly like it did when my father was growing the company. Now we have competition from all over the globe, and they move very fast."

Jason was holding his hand up like he was trying to get permission to speak, but Lilly was not going to stop.

"I need a team that can move quickly, and that means we all need to be working together, supporting each other and the company. We don't need cliques or individuals who seem to think they can run the company by themselves. "Now," Lilly said as she moved over in front of Jason, "are you willing to try this new approach?"

Jason stared at her for a second before backing up and said, "I came to your office thinking I could talk some sense into you, but apparently that's not going to happen. As you said, we need to work fast, and that is what I am going to do. If you would stop all these stupid meetings and time-wasting ideas, we may just survive. Now, I need to get back to work." With that, Jason turned and left.

Lilly now knew what she needed to do.

CHAPTER THREE

After Jason left, Lilly sat back down at her desk. She noticed she was shaking, and she was not sure if it was anger, frustration, or fear. She knew she needed more help. She picked up the phone and dialed the number on Steve's card.

"Hello, this is Steve."

"Hi, Steve, this is Lilly O'Hara. We met yesterday ..."

"Yes, Lilly, of course. How are you? How can I be of assistance?"

"I wish I could say I was fine, but I'm not. We had a terrible meeting today, and I would like to bounce some ideas off you and learn more about the rules of Solution-Building. I don't think I can wait until lunch next week with you and your wife. Do you have any time over the weekend?"

"Do you want to tell me a little about what happened? Then maybe I can understand where you are and how I can help." Lilly told him about the staff meeting and her encounter with Jason. She concluded, "I am going to have to dismiss one of them to get their attention, but I want to have something to follow up with too."

"All right, give me a few seconds to look my schedule." The sound muffled, and she could hear Steve talking with someone else. Then he came back. "How about Sunday, late afternoon?"

"Thank you. That would be wonderful. Same place?"

"Let's see, no, we are going to be across town," and he named a place. "At, say, 4:00?"

"I know the place, and I'll be there." She hung up. Then she called Mark and asked him to come over.

When Mark arrived, he immediately asked, "How are you doing? You looked really mad when you left. Everyone in the room was pretty shocked by what you said. Some were obviously angry, but they had enough sense to keep quiet other than The Triplets, especially Jason. He made it clear that he thinks you are flaky and not very competent."

"Is anyone taking it positively?"

"I think Allison may be, Stan from IT, and Ken from engineering—the ones you would expect. The rest are either too angry or too scared for me to read. I think Jason, Bill, and Donna are the biggest problems, and I have already been told that Jason is stirring up trouble, telling people all over the company what he thinks, which includes that you need to go and he needs to run the place properly."

"Well, that makes my choice a lot clearer and necessary. You may not know, but Jason and I met just a few minutes ago. Who in R&D would be a good replacement for Jason? I don't personally think it is the deputy director; he doesn't seem to have the personality even if he is a good scientist and researcher."

"Kelly Hong."

"Really? I have heard Jason say over and over again that she isn't that good as a scientist."

"She has more patents than anyone else in the department except Jason. He never liked her, but I wonder if that was jealousy. Anyway, he never tried to get rid of her because she is too critical to our new product efforts. But he would never promote her. I know her a little, and she has the ability to do the job, perhaps with a bit of hand-holding at the beginning."

"OK, I'll meet with her. Do you have a second choice? Just in case?"

"Not really, not in R&D. You remember when Jason was out of the country for three weeks and Bob assumed the administrative functions of the department? He hated it and said he was more comfortable just in focusing on his R&D work. However, I do think Bob would actually help Kelly since he knows he isn't the right person."

When Mark left, Lilly called Kelly and asked her to come for coffee. Lilly knew who Kelly was, knew she was a mother of an eight-year-old daughter and that she had a doctorate in physics from Stanford. Now she wanted to get to know her a little better.

When Kelly Hong walked in, Lilly saw a woman with a happy, open face wearing an expression of friendly curiosity. "Hi, Kelly. Would you like some coffee before we get started?" Lilly gestured toward a small table in the office and waited for Kelly to pour herself a cup and sit down.

They talked for a few minutes about family, and Lilly found herself liking Kelly more and more. Then they talked about Kelly's work at JOG. When Kelly got going, she started talking about new ideas she had for a number of products, including one that would rival or even be better than the rumored new Haze Systems product, their most serious competitor.

"And what does Jason think of these ideas?"

Kelly paused, looked unhappy, and said, "Jason ... he doesn't seem to consider them very interesting and keeps telling me to work on ideas he has." She hesitated a few seconds before adding, "The problem is that his ideas simply don't work."

"Really? Why?"

"Jason is very smart, but he doesn't seem to have stayed current with the latest developments, especially in nanotech. We need those advanced technologies if we are going to have a product that leapfrogs Haze."

"What do the others in the department think about that?"

"Those who aren't scared of Jason and know the technology agree that we need it. Jason just thinks it is a fad that will prove not as useful as it sounds, and he simply won't listen to us. So I work on it a little when I can fit it in around the tasks that Jason wants. A couple of others do the same, but we will eventually need additional support for prototyping and testing. I guess we hope that when Jason sees what we have he will realize its value."

Lilly asked a few technical questions and then thought for a short while before saying, "Jason will not be realizing the value of anything here after today. Kelly, I have decided to let him go, and I want you to take the position of director of R&D."

Lilly watched Kelly's face go through a number of expressions, ranging from disbelief to astonishment and, finally, realization of what was being offered. "I'm not even a section head, and there are others who have more management experience in the department. Why me? Why not one of them? Why not Bob?"

"Because I feel that you have what we need in terms of the technical expertise, and you have the respect of others in the company. To be honest, I don't see anyone else in the department who could do the job, and we do not have the time to go outside. Do you need time, say the weekend, to think about it? I want to make this change before Tuesday's executive meeting."

"Yes, I do need to think about it and should be able to tell you over the weekend, but I need your phone number."

Lilly watched as Kelly entered her number into her cellphone and then said, "Thanks, and I'll look forward to hearing from you." She thought about saying something about not talking with anyone at the company but kept her mouth shut. If she started out not trusting Kelly to know better, she shouldn't offer the position to her.

After Kelly left, Lilly called Mark, who was in the office within minutes. "How did it go?" he asked.

"She wants to think about it and will call me over the weekend. I hope she takes it, and I think she will. Meanwhile, I want you to prepare a termination letter for Jason. I want to give it to him on Monday morning, especially if Kelly accepts. After he leaves, I want the two of us to spend time with Kelly getting her up to speed for the Tuesday meeting."

Lilly spent the rest of Friday afternoon and Saturday in her office going over reports and plans. Kelly called at 2:15 Saturday afternoon.

"First, I want to thank you for not asking me to keep quiet about this. It told me you trusted me. That is an important part of my decision to accept the position. Jason never did trust me."

"That's great news, Kelly. Thank you. I think you will be great as the director and give us the best chance to be successful. Now, I plan to let Jason go first thing on Monday and make a general announcement to the company about the change. Have you thought about how you will handle the transition?"

"Yes, I have. That was part of the reason I didn't accept Friday night. I want to make some changes but also don't want to turn the department completely upside down, at least not right away. I want to take a few days to both think and discuss things with a few key people before making any changes, but I realize we have to get going quickly and can't afford to spend too much time reorganizing."

"Thank you, Kelly. We have a lot to discuss before your first executive committee meeting," said Lilly happily. "Meanwhile, I will call you before making the announcement on Monday so that you can be ready for it. I'll also let you see the announcement first so that we can all be on the same page when the questions come. Thanks again, and enjoy the rest of your weekend. See you Monday."

Lilly was both relieved and elated. She called Mark and gave him the news, discussing briefly what would happen early on Monday. Then she went back to work.

Sunday afternoon shortly before 4:00, Lilly walked into a place that locals simply called "The Courtyard." It consisted of small shops, boutiques, and a variety of places to eat, all housed on two levels built around a central courtyard complete with a fountain, trees, and potted plants. There were about two dozen tables of varying sizes where people could enjoy a quiet cup of coffee, a slice of hand-tossed pizza, or an ice cream.

She spotted Steve sitting at a small table in one corner of the courtyard under a decorative maple tree. Seated with him was a striking woman of indeterminate age. As Lilly approached, Steve rose to his feet.

"Ah, Lilly," he said warmly, "let me introduce you to my wife, Mara. Mara, this is the young woman I was telling you about who thinks I stepped out of a time machine."

"Well, I hope you didn't tell her where we keep it; she might try to borrow it. Hello, Lilly! How are you, dear?" Mara's greeting was delivered in a crisp British accent that could only be described as "posh."

"Hello, I'm glad to meet you. And thanks, both of you, for seeing me today. I'm kind of, well, desperate. And I need some more information about what Steve and I talked about on Thursday."

"Sit down, Lilly, please, and tell us about it." Steve waited until Lilly took a seat before sitting himself. The gesture seemed quaint and old-fashioned, but Lilly found it strangely comforting. "Why don't you start with what has happened since we met."

Lilly summarized her discussions with Mark, her searching of the Internet, and the meeting on Friday. She also told them about her decision to fire her director of R&D and replace him with Kelly.

As she talked, she found herself becoming a bit upset at the position she was in as a result of her meeting with Jason.

"And I will tell you something else. You filled my head with some wild idea that I could get my staff to work together, and then you walked away without telling me anything about how to do it. You teased me!"

Mara nodded her head and said, "He's always been that way. He drops some cryptic remark and expects people to read his mind. How much did he actually tell you?"

"He said the first rule of Solution-Building is that everyone has to agree to play by the same rules, but I don't know what the rules are!"

"Yes, infuriating," said Mara, "but in fairness to Steve, he is absolutely right, you know. Nothing we might possibly tell you will work unless everyone buys into that concept, as you tried to tell them already. While we cannot tell you the best way to accomplish that in your situation, you may have found one approach, albeit perhaps a bit extreme. I'll bet you got their attention, but please tell me something. Do you suppose your people will come to the next meeting more willing and ready to participate?"

"I certainly hope so, especially after the announcements I'll make on Monday. I hope they will understand that I am willing to fire people and will follow through on the threat I made. My father always said you should never make a threat you weren't prepared to back up with action, so maybe they will take things more seriously now. But the thing is, I would really not want to fire them all or even any more of them. That's why I called you."

Steve had been sitting quietly, listening to the conversation. Finally, he spoke up. "Lilly, of course we'll help, but there's one thing about the rules. Some are so obvious you will kick yourself—or me—when we tell you about them. In fact, Mara just gave you one of them whether or not you realize it."

Lilly looked puzzled. "What rule are you talking about, Steve?"

"The Second Rule, as are several more, is all about the attitude and behavior of the individuals within the group. It's about how they comport themselves and how they treat others, but it's more than that. It's also about how they view others as equal participants rather than antagonists that one must be artificially polite to. Here's the rule Mara was hinting at when she asked her question. For good measure, I'll give you another one to go with it.

RULE 2: You must come to the group ready and willing to participate.

"Yes, I know you might think your people are ready to participate, but are they really? Or are they just there to argue or perhaps to undercut someone else? Are they eager to hear new ideas? Do they have any new ideas of their own? Do they just sit there and sulk if they don't get their own way? Are they familiar with the needs of departments other than their own? Do they even care about other departments? Are they capable of seeing the bigger picture? These are all important questions to ask when gauging their readiness and willingness to participate in any meeting."

Not knowing how to respond to this barrage of questions and considerations, Lilly, to buy some time, asked the first thing that popped into her mind. "What is Rule Number 3?"

Steve smiled, "Well, you may not be ready, but at least you are willing. Fair enough."

RULE 3: Treat everyone in the group with courtesy and respect.

"Hmm," Lilly said, "I think I see the point of that one and how it is related to the first two. If you do not respect others, you won't listen to them and listening, really listening, requires courtesy, something a number of the members of my executive team don't seem to have, at least toward each other. And if you are discourteous and disrespectful toward others they will return the behavior." She paused a few seconds. "This also implies that you have to be courteous and respectful not just in meetings but all the time too. No one will believe you if you treat them badly everywhere else and then treat them courteously in a meeting. They won't trust you, and this is about trust, too, isn't it?"

It was Mara's turn to smile. "Exactly, Lilly. Trust is key to Solution-Building, whether about what to have for dinner or issues crucial to the survival of your company. Without it, and everything that goes with it, no group can make a decision that is other than the one the strongest personality in the room wants, but it goes a bit further than just trust: the people also have to like one another."

At this, Lilly snorted. "This group? Or any other group of egos like this? If liking is important, then this is a waste of time, isn't it? This bunch, or at least most of them, seem to take a great deal of delight in criticizing, antagonizing, and irritating each other, all to get their own ideas pushed to the front. Thinking they will actually 'like' each other is just … Oh! I think I get it. If people treat each other with actual respect and courtesy, they are more likely to discover things they like about each other. My best friend in college was someone I started out not liking but who was so courteous to me and everyone else I began to see her good qualities. We still are in contact, though not as often as I wish."

"Bravo," said Steve and Mara simultaneously. And Steve added, "That is why courtesy and respect are important, and you are absolutely right. Once we reorient ourselves to courteous and respectful treatment of others, we begin to treat them with trust and even begin to like them no matter how different from us they may be. But, and this is also important, courtesy and respect cannot be given unless you can receive it as well.

"Lilly, I see I need to elaborate on that a bit. Respect and courtesy are a two-way street. If you are not prepared to receive it, you cannot recognize it or return it, which leads us directly to:

RULE 4: Act as though the person whose respect is most important to you is watching how you behave.

"Do you remember the discussion we had the first time we met, when we were talking about fairness and impartiality?"

"Yes, you talked about justice, right?"

"I did, but the term is loaded, so I prefer to think of it as fairness and impartiality. You have seen people come to meetings determined to push their own agendas and ideas and unwilling to consider any other possibilities or suggestions. From what you have described at your executive meetings, that seems to be the case—everyone pushing their own agenda and unwilling to let go of it. This leads us directly into:

RULE 5: No personal agendas allowed.

55

Lilly said, "Let me see if I have these rules. I have written them down as I understand them." She showed Steve and Mara a piece of paper she had been writing on:

- **Everyone plays by the same rules**
- **You must come prepared and willing to participate**
- **Treat everyone in the group with courtesy and respect**
- **Act as though the person whose respect is most important to you is watching how you behave**
- **No personal agendas allowed**

"Do I have them right?"

"Yes, you do," said Steve.

"Are these all the rules? Just being polite and treating each other well seems like it will not lead to actually getting decisions made."

Mara said, "These are a set of behavioral rules covering the way people act both in the meeting as participants and toward each other. If the members of your executive committee cannot agree to and operate by these rules, the others won't help, but you are correct that they themselves will not lead directly to the results we want even though they are important to this process and will certainly make for better meetings and discussions."

"But there are two others that follow directly from those five and are perhaps the critical ones in this approach." Steve looked at Mara and said, "How would you put the next one?" "Well," said Mara, "how about:

RULE 6: Park your egos at the door or you don't get a seat at the table.

"This is the best way to state it that I have seen, considering the group you are working with. Does that make sense to you?"

"I think it does; actually I know it does. And that's where this all falls apart." Lilly shook her head and frowned. "I must have missed the part where I had to do the impossible. You have heard my description of this group. Do you honestly believe they will actually set their egos aside and suddenly play nice together?" She sat wondering if she had just wasted the last several days on something that had a near-zero probability of being useful.

"You said there was another one that was critical?" Lilly, once again, wondered if this was a waste of time but decided that she needed to hear this out. She was not sure she had any other alternatives that would work to save the company anyway.

"Yes," said Mara, "and that it is a direct consequence of leaving ego at the door. It is usually stated this way:

RULE 7: Once you put your idea or opinion out there, it no longer belongs to you.

"Perhaps you need to explain that to me a bit. I think I see what it is getting at, but, again, this is so different. Who does the idea belong to if not the person who puts it out there?"

Steve said, "That is perhaps the principle innovation of this approach. The idea, opinion, proposal, or whatever you call it now belongs to the entire group, which can then evaluate it critically, looking at its value, objectively examining its strengths and weaknesses in the context of the problem being solved and the entire body of ideas being considered."

"But if it's my idea, won't I be unhappy with other people poking holes in it? After all, if I have it and offer it up, why wouldn't I

57

think it is a really good idea? I wouldn't put out one I didn't think was good, would I?"

"No, you probably wouldn't," said Steve, "but if your ego is not involved, if it is left at the door as Rule 6 says, wouldn't you be able to listen to a critical evaluation with a more objective mindset? Remember that everyone else is supposed to be playing by this rule as well, and their ideas are subject to the same process. And further, remember the previous rules that are being followed, the ones that say we treat each other with respect and courtesy and have left our personal agendas in the trash bin. If all those rules are followed, the critical evaluation of ideas and opinions will not be contentious, rude, or nasty. Then you, the person who offered up the idea in the first place, can listen to the evaluation and see aspects you may not have considered, aspects that you may be happy to drop or modify. Or you may see why the idea may not be so wonderful after all. You may find yourself advocating for something else entirely after the ideas are examined in detail."

"You're right. This is a pretty radical innovation. It seems to me that this would be the hardest one to get people to accept. My experience is that people are pretty much wedded to their own ideas and don't take kindly to criticism, but I can see how it could work if the team all played by the first five rules. I bet it is difficult to get people used to this one."

"It is and it isn't," said Mara. "Gentle reminders are needed sometimes to make sure the first five rules are followed, and the entire group needs to learn to trust one another. Some take to it naturally, while others need encouragement, but when people see this actually work, they begin to understand and accept it. Then they want to use it."

"OK, so I put out an idea and it is subject to this process and the group decides not to use it. What if it WAS the right idea in the first place?"

"Hmm," said Steve, "well, I guess you could say that if it was the 'right' idea—and I'm not sure that any single idea is the only right one—and was not adopted, the results will quickly tell you that and you can change course. After all, you are not exactly starting from scratch if you have to go back and reexamine things, are you?

Our experience is that there is seldom a single right solution, and ultimately the one that works is often a synthesis of several, arrived at after consideration of all the ideas, but that synthesis cannot happen unless you carefully examine all the ideas and opinions no matter the source. This is another strength of this approach: you can put several good ideas together and make a great one. Then it truly is the group's solution and not one person's."

Lilly looked from Mara to Steve and said, "I think I understand this better, even if I am struggling with believing it can happen. What you are saying is that we cannot be married to our own ideas to the exclusion of all others."

"Exactly!" said Mara.

Steve smiled and nodded his head. "I think that sums it up pretty well."

Lilly said, "I am still concerned about getting everyone on my team to function by these rules, but if I can, you have convinced me that it has a good chance, and it will stop the useless rancor and bickering. But you said there are other rules?"

"There are, but unless these first seven are adopted, they don't have any place, really. They are more about what happens after we toss our ideas out to the group."

"Are you teasing me again? What are these other rules, and how many are there?"

Mara said, "I am not sure you need more rules yet until you get them on board with the first seven. Steve may be guilty of teasing again, but he is right this time. I think you have enough to consider for now. How do you think you will introduce these next six rules?"

With that change of topic, Lilly realized she would not get any more rules from these two. Well, she thought, they seem to know what they are talking about. She decided to be patient.

"I ... I'm not sure; that's a lot to hit them with at once. They have already seen the first one, of course, and you heard the reaction. My first thought is to do this one at a time, but I don't think the company has the time to do that." She thought a few seconds. "It seems to me that rules two to five are fairly closely related, and my first task is to get them to behave in a way that could be productive. Then I can put Rules 6 and 7 on the table. So I will start with a long meeting on Tuesday and lay out Rules 2 to 5, probably with some discussion. I have a few more questions about all seven of them, if you can spend the time."

"We can stay a while," said Mara, and Steve nodded. "But why wait until Tuesday? Oh, that's right, you have a lot to do tomorrow with moving your R&D head out. That will probably get a few others worried, don't you think?"

"Yes, I do have a lot to do, and you are right. His exit will raise a lot of questions and perhaps instill a bit of fear, and even respect,

in the rest. Now, if I may ask a question about the second rule
…"

They talked for another hour and a half before Lilly realized that
Steve and Mara were getting tired and probably had other things
to do besides talk to her about the issues at JOG. She decided she
needed a good night's sleep, too, and it was time to leave herself.

"Please forgive me for keeping you two out so long. It was very
kind of you to spend your Sunday evening with me, and I cannot
tell you how much I appreciate it or how much help this could be
to the company. Perhaps you will let me take you to dinner next
weekend?"

"We've enjoyed speaking with you and hope we are helping a bit,
and we would be happy to accept your invitation. Besides, there
are more rules to discuss, and they may also be difficult to accept
because they too represent a radical departure from the normal
process most groups use to make decisions."

"Like these won't be? What are they?"

"We should wait on that. Once we do discuss them with you and
explain the principles behind them, you will more than likely
agree that if your staff can buy into the first seven, the next ones,
even though they are unusual, do logically follow. "But," said
Steve when Lilly opened her mouth to protest, "we should stop
here because the next rules require agreement with the first seven
to fully understand their meaning. I perceive we are all tired, and
you have some long days ahead of you this week. Why don't we
plan to meet at," and he named a cozy little restaurant not far
from Lilly's home, "next Saturday at 1:00 for a midday meal and
be prepared to spend the afternoon talking about the remaining
rules?"

"OK," Lilly said, suddenly feeling more tired than she had thought, "that sounds good. And again, thank you both for all you are doing. I confess I have to wonder why you are willing to spend time with a total stranger helping her out of a very deep hole."

Steve looked at her with a slight smile and said, "Sometimes it is the right thing to do a service for someone who needs help. Remember that we are at The Corner Deli each Tuesday for lunch if you want to talk with us after your morning meeting."

"Thank you," Lilly said and paused for a minute. "We've discussed a lot of things today, and you obviously have implemented these rules successfully. I need to ask, who are you? I mean, I have never been around anyone that can so calmly gather information and support in order to move an organization forward. She pulled out Steve's card and said "your business card says 'Consultant.' What do you do?"

"Well, we work with an organization called Capacity Builders," said Steve, "It's a nonprofit that provides funding, guidance, and counseling to small businesses. We have the good fortune to work with several people who understand these rules we have been telling you about and use them every day, especially when critical decisions need to be made and carried out."

"When all this is over and hopefully running well, I think I would like to learn more about Capacity Builders," said Lilly, "and I suspect I will be seeing you for lunch on Tuesday."

CHAPTER FOUR

On Monday morning, Lilly came in early and noticed that Kelly was already in. She called and asked her to come up to the office. When Kelly arrived, Lilly gave her a copy of the announcement that would go out as soon as Jason was gone. She read it silently and nodded. They spoke for a few minutes, and then Kelly went back to the lab. Lilly called Mark. "Let's get this over with."

At 9 a.m., Lilly sat at her desk thinking about the last hour. She had known Jason, who had been with JOG from the beginning, since she was a teenager. He had been responsible for many of the company's advances, but for the past few months, he had been a brick wall, resisting any and all ideas not his own. He had to be moved not just out of the way but out of JOG completely; he could not be kept on in any capacity. And she had to do it herself, but she took Mark and the head of building security with her.

Jason did not accept it quietly or easily, but he left when he realized Lilly was in charge, serious and determined. The announcement had been made immediately at a short company meeting, and Kelly was introduced as the new head of R&D.

Lilly was relieved that Bob had stood up and supported the decision, offering his support to Kelly as she was moving into her new position.

Reaction was mixed. Everyone was surprised, but some looked relieved, while others seemed angry and confused. She noted that the heads of marketing and finance looked shocked, then angry and then, after the news sank in, actually afraid. They left the room together, quietly. Others stayed and tried to ask questions, but Lilly put them off, explaining that other changes, if and when they occurred, would be announced later. Then she returned to her office, told Pat to clear the calendar and let no one in except Mark for the afternoon, and then she closed her office door.

She decided to stay in her office the rest of the day since she did not want to continue to avoid answering questions and needed to think about how to introduce the next several rules of Solution-Building to the executive committee. Kelly would have to be briefed on the first rule, and she wanted to discuss with Mark—to "consult" with him (the thought brought a wry smile to her lips, her first real one of the day) about the next five rules and how to introduce them. She did not have time to make the introduction of the rules a lengthy process and felt she could depend on Mark to offer good suggestions and advice as well as support.

Kelly met with Lilly at about 10 a.m. "How is the move into the front office going?"

"Slowly. I have been boxing up Jason's books and noncompany papers so I can have some room of my own and, well, frankly it seems a bit intrusive into his life here. I am not sure what is the company's and what is his.

"Let security, IT, and HR handle it. They can sort through and get his personal stuff to him. I know it is a bit strange coming into an office with a lot of someone else's possessions, but I want you to concentrate on getting R&D organized so we can start getting back on track as soon as we can. Why don't you stay in your old office for a day or two until your new office is ready? Meanwhile, I wanted to bring you up to speed with where we are and what has been going on. I know the scuttlebutt has been out there, but I want you to have my version of things."

Lilly was prepared to spend the rest of the morning on it but quickly realized that Kelly was already well prepared. She had been meeting with Bob and the section heads and was considering how she would reorganize the department. She reiterated that she was not going to make immediate major changes, but she wanted to get some of the younger members of the department more directly involved in product design and improvement. Some of them, she told Lilly, were very bright and had some interesting ideas; she wanted them to put those ideas on the table so they could be considered by the department. She also wanted to start meeting with the engineering department regularly to discuss new ideas and how they could be implemented and had talked to Ken, head of engineering, about it already. In recent years, the company had hired some very promising young scientists and engineers. She and Ken wanted to understand some of the newer concepts coming out of the basic research team and how they could be applied to new products from JOG.

Lilly had the feeling that she had made the right choice and told Kelly so. Then she changed topics entirely.

"Kelly, I am changing the way we make decisions around here, as I told you on Friday. We already talked a little about this, but the other day I began the process by stating Rule Number 1: Everyone plays by the same rules. One of our biggest problems is that we have a room full of people pushing their own ideas and desires and doing their best to put others down. We need to be pulling together in the same direction instead of tearing ourselves apart. We need to choose a path and follow it, something this group is not doing, and I can't do it by myself. At the end of that meeting, I have to admit that I was hopping mad. I had asked how many wanted the company to succeed, and the response was hesitant and tentative from many of them. So, I gave them an assignment for the weekend: decide whether or not they still want jobs here. If they do, they will follow the rules I introduce. If they don't, they will either be fired or the company will fail." Kelly nodded, as if she already knew that, which she did.

"At tomorrow's executive meeting, I plan to introduce several more rules," said Lilly, "and so the meeting will be different from any you may have heard about."

"Actually, Ken told me what happened at the last meeting when we met right after the announcements this morning. He was very impressed and from what he said, he is on board."

"Oh," said Lilly, realizing that even though she had not expected this to happen, it seemed as though Kelly and Ken had already begun to work as part of the team. "Great, Kelly, and thanks for that feedback. Most of what I have heard has been negative."

"To be honest, there is a lot of that, too, but from what little I have heard so far, your stock has risen after you stood up to Jason on Friday. His carping and backbiting actually served to get people thinking about what you said about working from the same set of rules, and I think a number of people are becoming hopeful. What I was hearing on Friday afternoon was what others in the trenches had heard from their bosses, not from the execs themselves, so how much was accurate I don't know. The rumor I heard was that you were going to fire us all if we did not work a miracle, especially in R&D. After you and I met in the afternoon, I knew better, but there is still concern about the future of JOG."

"Well, perhaps a little worry is a good thing. I want people to consider the consequences of failure. After the meeting tomorrow, I hope the word can spread that we are not giving up, and if there is a way to succeed, and I believe there must be, we will all be working here for years to come."

"For what it is worth, a few of us, maybe a lot of us, in R&D believe that as well. I personally believe we can use some of the advanced technologies that are coming online to not just compete but again be the technological leader," said Kelly.

They talked a little while longer, and Kelly left, saying she would be looking online for some information about Solution-Building, assuming she had the time. Lilly called Mark.

The rest of the day Mark was in and out of Lilly's office as they discussed the rules Steve and Mara had given Lilly on Sunday. Lilly wanted the meeting to go as well as possible and felt that the approach they took to both introducing and explaining the next several rules was critical to their acceptance and actual use. She wanted the senior staff to understand that meetings would no longer be contentious at JOG. Some sort of structure and discipline was needed, and these rules would provide them.

Around midafternoon, Mark had to return to his own office. "I have a couple of paperwork items to get out, and they won't take more than fifteen minutes." He was gone almost an hour.

"Get distracted from your fifteen minutes of paperwork?" Lilly asked when Mark returned.

"Yes, actually, when I got to my office, there was a crowd wanting to see me. Most wanted to know who was next."

"Next?"

"To be fired. I think this morning's meeting scared a number of people, including the remaining Triplets. Or are they The Twins now, or The Terrible Twos?"

"They came to you themselves?" Lilly asked, slightly surprised.

"No, but since their admin assistants were first in line, it was pretty transparent. I decided that I could not speak for the CEO and told them the decision was not mine, and I was not privy to your thinking on the matter. They looked pretty glum when they left."

Lilly smiled, "Thanks for that one. It should keep those two concerned, especially since Jason was their ringleader." She thought a minute and then said, "Tomorrow's meeting is likely to be long, and since I think this is important, we probably need to start early before anyone gets themselves caught up in things. I am sending out an email to the execs telling them we start with a light breakfast at 7:30 a.m., and the food will be gone and the meeting will begin at 8:00 sharp." After she hit "send," she turned and said, "Now, back to your crowded office. Let's make it official: I haven't made up my mind yet about letting anyone else go. It will depend on their performance at tomorrow's meeting. Since that's the truth, it will be easy to keep the story straight."

Mark smiled and nodded. "OK, if I'm asked again, that's what I'll say. Now, we were discussing, I think, Rule Number 4 …" And they continued to talk.

When Lilly left that evening, she felt she had prepared as much as she could for the next morning and that she had prepared Mark as much as possible, given her own limited time to consider the rules. Mark, an experienced HR director who had been involved in many brainstorming sessions, had said something Lilly was still grappling with.

When Lilly had told Mark about **Rule 6: Park your egos at the door or you don't get a seat at the table**, Mark had looked surprised and expressed the same doubt as Lilly had when she first heard it. Later, after they had come to the conclusion that they would introduce and discuss Rules 2 through 5 at this first meeting and put off numbers 6 and 7 for a couple of days, he said, "I wonder if this crew is capable of showing enough maturity to deal with this approach in a constructive way."

Lilly had only replied that she hoped they would since they didn't have time to spend trying to do this slowly. What she was thinking and had not yet mentioned to Mark was that Steve and Mara had said the next few rules were the hard ones. *Yes,* she thought, *it is all about maturity, isn't it?*

As she entered her home, she also considered another subject. Mark, as she had expected, had asked Lilly where she was getting this material. Lilly hesitated some, but since she was a believer in honesty and could not think of a valid reason not to tell Mark, she said, "I have been discussing our issues with some outside consultants I know, and they advised me to introduce these rules myself." Mark was very curious about these consultants and asked if he could meet them as well. Again, Lilly had no valid reason to say no but wanted to think about it first and told Mark so.

Mark accepted that, of course, but Lilly could feel his skepticism and asked, "How do you think Jason and the others would have acted if I had brought in two unknown people to tell us what to do?"

"Badly, probably embarrassing the rest of us. Then you may have had to fire them all."

CHAPTER FIVE

illy arrived at 6:30 Tuesday morning and saw a number of cars in the lot, recognizing some of them as belonging to members of the executive team. Mark had just arrived and was getting out of his car; they walked in together.

"The food will arrive at about 7," said Mark, "I hope you don't mind that I asked Pat to pick it up on the way in."

Lilly walked into the conference room at precisely 7:30 and found several of the execs already there, preparing bagels and pouring coffee. "Good morning," she said to Stan from IT, Allison from sales, and Jim from production. As they were responding, Kelly and Ken came into the room. Mark followed a few seconds later and then Brad from legal. There was a bit of chit-chat while people got some food and drink, mostly about family and the weather. Finally, at about 7:45, Donna, the CFO, and Bill, the head of marketing, came in. Both were wearing scowls, but they got some breakfast and sat down at the table with the others.

Mark and Lilly looked at one another, and the expression on his face reflected what Lilly was thinking: *this is a record; the whole team is early for a meeting.* Lilly smiled and said, "Well, since everyone is here early, we can go ahead and start."

Lilly went on before anyone could comment. "We have a lot to cover in our discussion of the rules we will use for Solution-Building and will not get through everything in one meeting, so this is the first of several we will have over the next week." She looked around the room, but no one said anything. She felt tensions begin to rise.

"OK, first, let's go back to your homework assignment. I will ask again: who among you wants this company to survive and prosper? Raise your hands if you do, please."

This time all the hands in the room went up, several before even Lilly raised hers. "Well, I'm glad to see us all on the same page for a change," she said to a round of nervous laughter. "I plan to introduce and discuss four more rules today, but I want to do a couple of other things first. One concerns Jason." There was complete stillness in the room. Lilly thought, *I've never seen this group so silent.*

"This is something I want you all to understand, since I am quite serious about the survival of this company. I did not fire Jason thoughtlessly. After our meeting on Friday, I met privately with him to try to get him on board with me, but it became clear that he would not participate in any way in a different process that was not his own, especially not the Solution-Building approach I am introducing. I made the decision to let him go."

She looked around the room and saw grim expressions on nearly every face. "This is not an apology. I was given responsibility for this company by my father, someone all of you knew, and I take that responsibility seriously. Any of you who feel the same way

Jason did had better see me either during a break or after this meeting to discuss your future with JayOGrafix. I hope I have made myself clear because I do not want to have to let anyone else go. We have a good team here. This is a critical time, and we have to work together."

"Now, speaking of the team, I want to formally welcome our newest member, Kelly, the new head of R&D. She has my full confidence and the support of the R&D department. She has accepted that responsibility knowing the challenges we face. Welcome, Kelly."

Kelly nodded and, to a chorus of welcoming comments, said, "Thank you, Lilly."

Before any other comments could be made, Lilly went on, "Now for the second subject:

RULE 1: Everybody plays by the same rules.

"You all had a weekend and more to think about it. What does it mean?" She looked around the room at a mix of startled and blank expressions. "Come on, don't tell me that a room full of intelligent people never even thought about this over the weekend!"

Everyone seemed to be waiting for someone else to speak first. After a few seconds, Ken spoke. "You summed it up in the last meeting: we all have to be on the same page."

Bill suddenly spoke up. "I see it sort of like this: if I am playing checkers and you are playing chess, even though the game boards are identical, the rules, strategies, and even pieces are different. We can't play each game on the same board simultaneously. Nothing can happen."

Lilly was pleased that Bill, who usually just attacked whomever had spoken, had come up with this analogy. "Bill, thank you for a great example of why we have to all play by the same rules. Any other thoughts?" She looked around the room.

Allison said, "You called us a good team a few minutes ago. Teams, at least sports teams, have to work together to win games. To use something like Bill's example, if you have two teams on a field, one playing soccer and the other rugby, it would be a mess, wouldn't it? Actually, maybe a better example would be having a team of soccer players except for a couple who were playing by rugby rules. Not much of a chance of actually winning against a team all playing the same thing." There were murmurs of agreement around the table.

Bill then said, "All this is well and good, but I still don't see where we are going with this. You said we were going to discuss more rules today. How many are there? Where are you getting this? How many more meetings are you planning to use with these rules anyway? We know we have a critical situation, and yet we are spending time discussing rules? I don't see how this is supposed to help."

Lilly held up her hand. "Whoa, Bill, please slow down. I will try to answer some of your questions but will start with the last comment first." She paused, thinking she was happy to deal with the issue earlier rather than later.

"How many times have we met to try to develop ideas and strategies to save this company in the past few months? Two dozen? More? And what was the result? Gridlock, infighting, blame-throwing, and shouting matches. Any argument with that characterization?"

Stan from IT said, "You forgot frustration." There was a smile on his face, but Lilly knew he was serious. How could anyone not be frustrated?

"Yes, there was certainly plenty of that for all of us, I'm sure, but there was no real discussion of the problem and how we could work as a team to fix it. We need a different approach, an attitude adjustment that will allow us to do something positive and actually work together to get out of this mess. Does that help?"

Bill said, "And you think these rules will do the trick?"

"Bill," said Ken, "for one thing, we need to hear and probably discuss these rules before any of us can answer that. But what else do we have? The simple fact is that anything is better than where we are now, don't you think?"

"Well, yes, that is true, but this sounds … I don't know, like some sort of formula, and I just don't believe in formulas for making decisions." There was an echo of agreement with that statement from around the table, but it did not seem to Lilly that it indicated trouble … yet.

"Ken is right that until we actually discuss these rules no one can say whether or not they may help us, but if you will bear with me, you will see that they are really about a different way of thinking through issues to solve problems and make decisions based on the value of the ideas, every idea, no matter who first puts it on the table," said Lilly. "I think, Bill, that once we all see and have a chance to discuss these rules, you'll see that rather than being a formula, they will actually help us avoid the formulaic."

"As to how many there are, you will find that out as we go on, but it is not a lot, nine or ten. You asked where I am getting them.

I am working privately with a consulting group that uses this approach."

"Why don't they come and give them to us?" asked Allison.

"These have to be *our* rules, not something imposed, given, by some outside source. I know I am giving them to you, but I intend for us to actually discuss them and come to agreement on their implementation for the sake of the company and for everything we in this room have worked for over the years."

"Before we continue with the next several rules, are there any more comments or thoughts on rule number one?" Lilly then pushed a button on her JOGpad, and the JOGboard behind her lit up with:

RULE 1: Everybody plays by the same rules.

"Now, I want to see another show of hands. I want to know how many of you intend to follow this rule without further question."

Over a period of a couple of seconds, everyone raised a hand. Several, including Bill, Donna, and to Lilly's surprise Brad, were the last to raise their hands but seemed unhappy. "All right," she said, "I am going to accept that as a commitment from all of you. I expect you all to keep that commitment." She looked each member of the group in the eye as she made that statement.

"The food is gone, except for coffee and water, so take a couple of minutes to refresh your drinks or use the restroom, and we will get started with the next rule." She looked around the room and was pleased that everyone was paying attention. *They probably think I'm looking for something to catch them on and fire them,* she thought. She really hoped this would be a turning point. She got up and began to fill her cup with some fresh coffee.

After everyone had refreshed their drinks and returned, she touched her JOGpad to reveal:

RULE 2: You must come to the group ready and willing to participate.

Not a sound was made, so Lilly decided to just ask questions. "Donna, what does this rule mean to you?"

"Well, I think it means showing up, right? I mean we are here and willing to talk."

"I don't want to sound like Jason," Bill interrupted, "but we have a lot of work to do. Why can't we just get through all these new rules and get back to work?"

"You're right, Bill. We do have a lot of work, but as we discussed the other day, we can't continue to plod along like we've been doing. I really believe there is a better way of communicating and making decisions, and if we don't take action now, I fear we will fail and this company will no longer exist." She looked around the room, and it seemed that everyone was ready.

"Now, let's talk about this rule. To me, it means you not only show up, but you are an active participant. The best decisions are made when everyone participates. Withholding an idea, for whatever reason, could potentially be detrimental. The things you say, even the wild ideas, may cause someone to think of something else. What if that idea then spawned a major improvement or even a new product line? We all need to be active participants. We all know each other, what our specialty areas are, and through this process, great things may happen, especially if we are all using our full expertise and creativity."

"So, is this a brainstorming thing?" asked Bill. "We have all been through this type of thing before, and as far as I can tell it only works to solve one thing."

"This is beyond that," Lilly said. "What we are trying to achieve here is a whole new way of doing things. Brainstorming is blurting thoughts out, writing them down on a board, and then picking through them. This is much more. This is an open discussion where everyone can feel safe without being attacked. Everyone needs to feel comfortable with jumping in. We all know people who are quiet, non-joiner types. If you are one of those, you need to feel comfortable enough with the group that you can speak your ideas and not worry about getting shot down."

She decided now would be the best time to reveal Rule Number 3. She touched her JOGpad again to show:

RULE 3: Treat everyone in the group with courtesy and respect.

"What we just discussed really needs to have this rule for support. We all have good ideas and bad ideas, at least we think so. Maybe someone else sees your ideas a different way. Yes, there are ideas that just won't work, but maybe an open discussion of that unworkable idea will lead to the lightbulb going off in somebody's head. Maybe the next industry-changing idea is right here ready to come out, but if we don't let it, then we may go the way of the dodo bird."

"Okay," Bill said, "if I understand you correctly, you want us to throw out ideas, listen, and be supportive. I get it, but how is that going to work? I mean we have had very lively meetings in the past when it felt like someone was going to explode." Others in the room chimed in on that with grunts and chuckles.

Donna spoke up, "I have tried to offer ideas in the past, and they just get shot down without discussion. How can you be sure that won't happen again? I also know some people just never speak up."

Mark was ready for this, so he decided to chime in, "You all know me and that I rarely speak up unless it is a topic regarding some compliance issue, but I think I like this new way. You know, I think we are doing it already. So far we are having a good discussion without anyone yelling or stomping out of the room." That made everyone laugh, since they had all seen that happen before. "I really see this as a great opportunity to work together without the risk of being ridiculed."

"He's right," said Lilly. "We need to move past the old ways. We should not insult any idea or argue with each other. No matter how silly an idea is or how off-topic it is, it is still valuable. This is also not a competition to see who comes up with the most ideas; no one is keeping score. The real score is when we all succeed and the company grows."

Lilly looked around the room and continued, "Now, I want you to think about the first three rules, how they are related to each other, and how you are going to apply them in not just our meetings but elsewhere as well. Ah, time for a break. Please be back in half an hour."

When they all came back, exactly thirty minutes later, Lilly had rearranged the JOGboard to have rules one through three in a small box in the upper left-hand corner, leaving the rest of the board empty. She said, "Now we have a set of rules, or perhaps principles, that are a foundation for others. You have all agreed to play by the same rules, be prepared to participate, and to treat each other with respect. You had a half hour to consider these rules, and I suspect have some further thoughts. Now is the time to bring them out."

Silence followed, and Lilly decided to see who would talk first, so she waited.

After a few seconds in which people were looking around at each other, Kelly finally spoke up. "Well, this is my first meeting, and even though you," she nodded toward Lilly, "briefed me on the first rule, I haven't had the weekend to consider it, but I could offer my first reaction to how these work together."

"Please do. Perhaps we can get some fresh insights," said Brad drily. Then he added, "Excuse me, Kelly. In view of the new Rule 3, perhaps my tone should have been better."

"Thanks, Brad. It seems to me that these first three are about attitude and intent—an attitude that we have to play as a team, which means that, as any team that wants to win, we have to work together for a common overall goal. Each of us and our staff has a role, a part to play, but the overall goal is to once again be a leader in our product lines. We all have our own expertise, and no one department or function is more important than another." Several people started to interrupt, but Kelly held up her hand and calmly said, "Please let me finish. I would love to hear what you have to say after I am done. By that I mean that the R&D group can come up with some pretty nifty stuff and can even make a crude version, but unless Ken's engineering staff can clean it up and make it simpler, Jim and production will not be able to manufacture it, at least not affordably, right?" Both Jim and Ken nodded, and she continued.

"Then we need to sell it. I used to hear that if you built a better mousetrap the world would beat a path to your door. I said that to my dad once, and he just laughed and told me that first the world needed to know you had a better mousetrap and second, they needed a map to be able to find that door. That means marketing and sales, and then we need financial management and all the other business stuff I guess I have to learn about but know we need."

Allison spoke up. "That seems to cover the first two rules pretty well, but what about the third one? It seems a bit, well, distant from the first two."

"I thought that, too, but then I realized it was the one about attitude—our attitude toward each other and maybe even toward ourselves, as we use the rules, whatever they turn out to be."

"I'm not sure I fully follow that," said Bill. Several others nodded agreement.

"Well, here's how I thought it out. Do any of us like to work with people who are rude and unpleasant toward us? I don't think so, and it isn't just me. I am new to this team, but I have seen how you others have interacted outside these meetings. It used to be like any other group of people: some got along better than others, but you all seemed to at least be polite and civil around the building. None of us, at least among the people I work with, could miss the change over the past few months. To be blunt, it was for the worse. All of a sudden there were snarls and nasty comments, publicly, where we almost never saw or heard them before. It seemed that all of you hated each other. In fact, my hesitation when Lilly offered me this job mainly grew out of my fear that I was stepping into a mess, and I was not interested in, frankly, becoming what I was seeing in the rest of you: unhappy and angry."

"Ouch!" said Stan. "You don't pull your punches, do you?" But he was smiling, at least slightly, and his tone was more bantering than anything else. Other comments were heard, but some were definitely angry. Lilly decided to step in.

"For one, I don't believe any of you, if you think about it, will actually say Kelly is wrong in that assessment. I have known some of you for years and have watched the attitudes toward one another here deteriorate steadily since Dad died. Kelly is on the right track, though, in her realization that Rule 3 is about attitude toward one another. Does anyone want to argue that the rancor, arguments, and angry words have done anything to help us?"

She looked around the room. "Well?"

She was surprised to see Bill indicate he wanted to say something. "I admit to, and apologize to Kelly for, being angry about her characterization. Perhaps that comes from realizing that she is right. A bit harsh, but maybe we need that just now. I agree that it's hard to listen to someone you are mad at or have lost respect for, and I also agree that all of us need to find a way to get on board. It's just that, well, some nasty things have been said here, and it is hard to see how we can change our attitudes quickly."

Mark said, "Do you think you can?" The room was silent and Lilly, not expecting the question, waited, hoping for a positive answer. She got it.

"Yes, I am sure I can, but it may require some effort to forget— no, set aside—some of the things that we have heard here. And before you ask, yes I will make the effort."

Lilly let her breath out. "Thanks, Bill. Are there any other comments?"

There were, but mainly along the same lines, and she let the conversation go on for a few minutes before standing up, asking if anyone needed a break. They took five minutes, and when everyone was back, Lilly went on.

"Now for Rule Number 4." She reached down, and the JOGboard displayed:

RULE 4: Act as though the person whose respect is most important to you is watching how you behave.

As the words appeared on the JOGboard and everyone had a chance to read them, there were several reactions:

"What in the world does that have to do with anything else?"

"My old advisor will never be in this room!"

"It is not enough to treat everyone in the room with respect, but now we are supposed to pretend someone else is standing there watching? How do we do that?"

And a few more. Lilly let it go on for a few seconds and then held up her hand. The room went quiet. "OK, let's talk about this for a minute. Does anyone have an example of something they have said or done that they immediately regretted because of the people that were present?"

To Lilly's great surprise, Donna raised her hand and said, "I used to help my dad during the summers. He was a master carpenter." Reactions around the table indicated that others were just as surprised. No one had ever seen Donna in anything other than smart business attire, with perfectly cut and polished nails and coifed hair.

"I never knew that, Donna," said Lilly, thinking that she really should not stereotype anyone. She wondered who else had unexpected sides to their personalities and experiences.

"Let me ask you a question. It may be a bit nosey, and you don't have to answer, but would your father have fit into the description of someone whose respect is most important to you?"

Donna looked a bit startled but said, "Well, yes, I loved my dad, and since I was an only child he taught me a lot, not just about carpentry but also what it meant to do a really professional job of any task. So I always tried to please him. Yes, he would be the one standing in this room, by this rule. Uh, why?"

Instead of answering the question, Lilly said, "So you did a lot of carpentry work for him. Did you ever whack yourself with a hammer or drop something on your foot, something that was painful and made you react in some way that was inappropriate or that he did not approve?"

Donna smiled uncomfortably. "Yes, a couple of times. Once I hit my thumb with a twenty-ounce hammer." There was a chorus of "Ouch!" from the group. "Ouch is right! I tore off my thumbnail, and it not only hurt like crazy, but I bled like a stuck pig."

"What did you do then?" asked Lilly.

Donna looked embarrassed and said, "Without even thinking, I let out a string of words that were pretty common at school. Dad had never heard anything like that from his little girl's mouth, and he stared at me with a hurt expression that I have never forgotten. I apologized profusely, but he only said that he had never heard a woman say anything that graphic in his life. I don't think he ever forgot it, and I did my best never to do anything like that again. I think I see what this rule is getting at: if I wouldn't say something in front of Dad, maybe I shouldn't say it in front of anyone."

Kelly said, "I would add any behavior to that, Donna. Gestures, expressions, actions, anything I wouldn't want my eight-year-old to do or say. In fact, when I am driving with her, I have to be careful how I react to other drivers. All it took was one shocked 'Mama!' when I wasn't thinking to convince me of that." The whole room, including Lilly, stared at Kelly; no one had ever heard her raise her voice, much less say something angry.

Lilly said, "Two good examples, with the added bonus of learning something new about two of our colleagues. Does anyone else have something to add?"

Allison said, "This is definitely one of the behavioral rules, along with Rule 3. I think I see its purpose. Our meetings have been long sessions of people criticizing each other and sneering at ideas, throwing insults, and generally making enemies of each other. Maybe if we treated each other better we can make the meetings more productive and useful. The idea of each of us pretending someone important to us is in the room who we do not want to disappoint is a bit kooky, maybe, but it will change the dynamic. Maybe each of us should picture who that person is and let that image help us. I know who I am thinking of and have no intention of saying, and I bet all of the rest of you do as well."

Lilly let the group be silent for a few seconds and then said, "Thank you, Allison, that was well put. I, too, know who that person is for me. Any other comments before we move to Rule 5?" There were a few head shakes, but no one actually responded. Lilly touched her JOGpad, and the JOGboard again changed. Rule 4 joined the box in the upper left-hand corner, and in the center was:

RULE 5: No personal agendas allowed.

Lilly let that sink in, and when no else spoke up said, "I saw this cartoon recently, and I thought it was relevant to this rule." She touched a key on her JOGpad.

A cartoon appeared. It showed a room of people having what could only be a meeting, much like this one. The person at the head of the table said, "Before we start the meeting, I want to take a few minutes to reflect on our hidden agendas."

Lilly said, "This is one of the biggest issues we face: hidden agendas. Does anyone disagree with that?" No one said a thing for about five seconds, and then Brad said, "I would bet we all agree with that statement. I would add that it is always the other guy's hidden agenda that is the problem, not our own."

"And what do hidden agendas do to a meeting or, as we have been trying to do, an effort at solving a problem?" asked Lilly. She looked around the room, making eye contact with each participant.

Jim was the first to respond. "They get in the way."

"How?"

"Well, for one, if you have your own agenda and want to see it carried out, you won't listen to anyone else's ideas or suggestions and will even find ways to attack it. Just like we have seen for weeks. For instance, Jason ..."

"I don't want to bring up people who are not here to defend themselves, please," Lilly interrupted.

"Sorry," said Jim, "but as I said, we saw that a lot. There were … others here who also had their own agendas …"

He was interrupted again, this time with a chorus of "WHO had agendas?" "And you didn't?" Lilly thought the meeting might just fall apart right then and there, so she held up her hand and said, loudly, "Stop it!" The room fell silent, and all faces turned toward her, a number of them angry.

"I have two things to say here. One is, remember Rule 3," and she pointed to the JOGboard. She then highlighted Rule 3 in the upper left-hand box: Treat Everyone in the Room with Courtesy and Respect. "The other is that I expected you to be honest with both yourselves and each other. You all know that hidden, and perhaps not-so-hidden, agendas have been a major problem with every meeting we have had. Many of you have been pushing yours at all the meetings. Before any of you climb onto your high horse on this, think about this bit of information: everyone has thoughts, ideas, and suggestions. This is what our personal agendas are composed of, and these thoughts, ideas, and suggestions, all of them from everyone, are absolute requirements for a truly meaningful and successful discussion and consultation that will take us forward. But the dark side of personal agendas is that we think, or tend to think, that our ideas are the good ones and our suggestions are the intelligent ones, and we are so convinced of this that we close our minds to anything else. Since our ideas and thoughts are the good ones, they MUST be the only way to go. When we are engaged in that thinking, we look for excuses to put down anything and anyone else. The agendas we shouldn't bring to our meetings are the ones that say we have the only 'right' answer and we have to get everyone else to agree to it and are willing to make certain no other options are adopted. That is what I have seen ever since we started trying to do something about the situation, the mess, we find ourselves in right now, and it has led to nothing but a lot of arguing and stagnation. In my opinion, it is going to sink us unless we can get them out of the way."

Jim said, "Uh, I'm sorry I opened my mouth."

"I'm not," said Mark suddenly. "Actually I am surprised at the denial going on here. I have heard all of you complain about other people and their inability to see anything but their own ideas. Often, two people are making that complaint about each other at the same time. How does that differ from not being able to see past their own hidden agendas? We all need to accept that this has been a major part of the mess of the last several months and agree with this rule; we all have to drop our personal agendas and agree to do what is best for the company and stop worrying about only our own selves. Or none of us will have jobs, and soon."

Gradually, most of the angry expressions softened as the group began to absorb what Mark had said. There were still a couple of people who looked angry, though, so Lilly added, "Those of you who think you do not have your own agendas need to take some time to think about this one. Remember, personal agendas are tied into the ideas we have as well as our own desires for position, influence, authority, all those things related to personal ambition. All of us have ambitions or we would not be as successful as we are, but now we need to put those personal ambitions aside. Or perhaps we need to redirect, or reorient, them to a much broader goal. We need to make it our personal desire to do what will help this company not just survive but thrive. As

Mark said, otherwise there won't be any jobs for any of us, and then where will your personal agendas have gotten you?"

Lilly put her hands over her eyes for a few seconds and then smiled and said, "I have had about enough for today. You might say I am about ruled out." A chorus of groans sounded, and Ken said, "If you are going to pun like that, I agree!" This was followed by some laughter and a few words of agreement.

"OK, there are more rules, and I want to meet again Thursday morning to both review what we discussed today and to introduce the next two rules, which follow directly from number five." She touched a key on her JOGpad, and the JOGboard went blank. She nodded to everyone and then left the room.

CHAPTER SIX

"Well, that's what has happened the last two days, and frankly I am not sure exactly where we are now. I plan to introduce Rules 6 and 7 on Thursday, but then what?" She looked at Steve and Mara, and they sat quietly for a few moments.

Lilly had left the building after the meeting, partly because she wanted to meet with these two and get an outside view of what had happened since Sunday, and partly so that she could avoid questions from anyone about what was going on. Sunday seemed like a long time ago now. When she arrived at The Corner Deli, she spotted them at the table where she had met Steve only a week ago; she ordered a sandwich and iced tea and then joined them. After a few minutes of greetings and general chit-chat, Mara asked how things had gone, suggesting Lilly be as detailed as she needed to be in the telling. Lilly talked for nearly twenty minutes.

"So you have introduced the first five rules. Things seem to be going well from what you have said, don't they?" Steve asked.

"Steve, I am not sure. I think they are going well, but it seems too easy. This is a group that couldn't even agree on what time it was just a couple of weeks ago, and ..."

"And now they seem to be at least willing to try to work together?" Mara added.

"I would like to think so, but I am not sure I believe it."

Steve looked at Lilly and said, "Don't you think it is possible that the firing of one of them got the rest of them to thinking that you were serious? I will admit that it seems easy, but is it possible that they are actually giving it a chance?"

"I don't know," said Lilly. "Maybe, but I don't believe some of them were actually serious about it. Certainly not very enthusiastic. I wonder if I should have given them another homework assignment. To think through those first five rules and be prepared to continue the conversation about them on Thursday. Or maybe I'm just being paranoid."

"Maybe," said Steve. He and Mara looked at each other, and then Mara said, "We have seen the reactions you are having before. I hope we did not imply that any of this would be easy; it isn't ever easy to get people to change their very way of thinking about anything, much less something that requires them to set aside their egos, their ingrained ways of doing things. And some people simply cannot do it at all."

"Are the ones you are concerned about Jason's friends?" asked Mara.

"They are the ones I am most concerned about, even though I would call them convenient allies rather than friends. But all of these people are pretty high ego types, so I am not sure of a couple of others yet as well. I know Mark is on my side and Kelly, probably Ken and Stan, but as for others, I don't think so yet. Am I going too fast?"

Steve said, "Perhaps it is a bit fast, but from what you have said you don't have the time to do this gradually. Besides, sometimes radical changes in procedure are best done quickly. Kicking over the apple cart is one way to get people to think about a better way to get them to market."

"Let's hope you don't have to kick that cart over too many times," said Mara. "What do you plan to do next?"

"I planned to let these first rules soak in for another day before we meet again on Thursday. Then I will bring out Rules 6 and 7. I was thinking of doing a couple of things to perhaps throw them off guard and, I hope, help them to consider seriously the idea of cutting their egos out of the process. Can I bounce some ideas off the two of you? I know we have been here a while and you probably have to go, but I would like your thoughts on some approaches."

"Yes, Mara has to be somewhere, but we have a little more time before she has to leave. Please tell us what you are thinking."

Lilly outlined something she had been thinking about since first hearing about:

RULE 6: Park your egos at the door or you don't get a seat at the table.

Steve and Mara listened, nodded, and finally Mara said, "That is a bit dramatic, but it will get their attention, I'm sure." They asked some questions and made some suggestions to Lilly before they left.

As they turned to leave, Steve said, "Do you want to talk again after your Thursday meeting? We are free this weekend."

"Uh, yes, I would like to talk about how things go and, perhaps more importantly, you said there are more rules, and they are going to be the hardest. I would like to learn about them."

"Oh yes, those others. We may need a bit more time than just a lunch. Do you have an extra block of time on Saturday afternoon when we meet?"

Lilly decided she would make the time, and they reaffirmed the plan to meet at noon on Saturday. Then Steve and Mara left the deli. Lilly sat for a while and thought before returning to the office. She decided to keep her plans to herself, to not even tell Mark what she planned to do.

<hr />

The rest of Tuesday and Wednesday went by in a blur for Lilly. She was closeted in her office most of the time and had a few meetings with individual execs to keep communication going, and, frankly, to keep them thinking about the previous meetings. She did not like to think she was keeping them worried, but she knew she was and decided not to worry about it herself. She also did a lot of planning on her own and prepared the materials she was going to need for the next meeting.

CHAPTER SEVEN

Lilly arrived at the small conference room twenty minutes early that Thursday morning. After checking the room itself to make sure no one had snuck in ahead of her, she went back into the hallway to stand guard. This was not the management team's usual meeting place but was close to her office. This proximity made it somewhat easier for her to do a little setup late the previous evening. She had placed a small table to one side of the doorway and set what appeared to be an old wooden ballot box on it, the kind of box with a hinged lid and a slot in the top in which to insert one's vote. Her final bit of preparation had been to send out an email late last night informing everyone of the change in location. Now she waited.

Stan Hadley was the first to arrive about five minutes later. He was the CIO at JOG and, as far as Lilly could tell, seemed moderately supportive of her efforts. She noticed he was carrying the ridiculous oversized coffee mug he always drank out of, the one that looked more like a tankard than a cup. He affectionately called it his "think tank."

"Hi, Lilly. Can we go in, yet?"

"Not yet, Stan. We're going to wait out here until everyone arrives. Then we're all going to participate in a symbolic act of sorts."

"Like a blood pact or something?"

"Sort of. You'll see. The rest should be coming along any minute now."

As if on cue, the rest of the team arrived within the next few minutes. Clearly, none of them wanted to be late. Lilly took a quick head count to make sure everyone was there and then got their attention.

"Good morning, all. I have something for each one of you. Please don't open them until I've handed them all out."

Lilly took a stack of envelopes from the side table. A person's name was neatly typed on each one. She handed them out to the members of the team and kept one for herself, which she now waved in her hand.

"Don't worry, I have one too. OK, let's open them up."

Lilly took a look at the contents of her own envelope. It was a 3x5 index card on which the words *Lilly's Ego* had been typed across the top. About an inch lower down on the card was a signature line. Each person assembled had been given a similar card.

"If you want to attend this meeting, then you're going to have to do what I do." She took one of several pens that were on the table next to the ballot box and signed her name on the index card. Holding it up briefly for all to see, she then inserted it in the box. "Everybody got it? OK, then." She turned and crossed the threshold into the meeting room, taking up station just inside the room. From there she could observe each person sign and insert his or her card in the box before entering the room and taking a seat.

Everyone took their seats without the usual light conversation that preceded meetings. Once everyone was seated, Lilly made her way to the head of the table and sat down before addressing them.

"First of all, I'd like to thank you for participating in this little piece of amateur theatrics. And having seen the looks on some of your faces when I passed out the envelopes, I think I should probably apologize. Apparently some of you thought I was handing out notices of termination. Sorry about that. My intention was for this symbolic act to signal the beginning of a new habit for all of us."

Like all the conference rooms in the building, this one was equipped with a JOGboard that hung on the wall behind her. In fact, it was one of JOG's own models, the SVB-207, which worked seamlessly with the JOGpad she had brought with her today. She tapped her JOGpad, and the JOGboard display came to life.

"This new habit is going to be the next rule for our consultations together, and it's the first rule we're going to talk about this morning."

Lilly tapped an icon on her JOGPad, and the display changed behind her.

RULE 6: Park your egos at the door or you don't get a seat at the table

"I guess the first thing we should probably discuss is what we mean by *ego*, at least in so far as our rule is concerned. So I looked up the word in the dictionary last night. In fact, I looked in several dictionaries, and I was mostly disappointed by the definitions that were given. They were either philosophical or metaphysical or psychoanalytical definitions that are, frankly, useless for our purposes. However, good old *Webster's Third Unabridged* did include one short and simple definition that works: SELF. Now, if we use this definition, the question then becomes: how do we leave ourselves behind when we come to a meeting? What does that imply? What are we really parking at the door? Anyone?" Lilly looked around the table expectantly.

"Stan? You look like you have something to say."

"Uh, sure, OK. Well, I was just doing a quick bit of word association. I mean, I assume what we want to leave behind are negative things associated with self, so I'm thinking of words like self-interest, self-centered, self-serving, and uh, selfishness?"

"Don't forget self-righteous, Stan." This last comment came from Donna, along with a rare smile. Lilly had always felt that Stan was one of the few people at JOG that didn't annoy Donna. In fact, now that she thought about it, she remembered that Stan and Donna occasionally played racquetball together.

"What about self-esteem?" asked Lilly. "Is that a good or bad thing to bring to a meeting?"

Donna apparently had nothing further to add to the conversation at this point and looked away from Lilly. Ken, however, was happy to jump in.

"Well, everybody needs it, and everybody feeds it. I guess the trick is to not overfeed it or you'll become full of yourself." Ken seemed quite pleased by his turn of phrase, but his smile began to fade when no one else responded. Lilly, however, thought she saw a great opportunity to move this discussion along, so she prompted him with a follow-up question.

"Interesting imagery, Ken. What happens when you become full of yourself? Not you, specifically, but anyone."

Ken persisted. "Hmm, good question. I guess I was just thinking in terms of self-esteem being kind of a synonym for ego, and that everybody needs a certain amount of self-esteem to be emotionally healthy and all, but like so many things which are good in moderation, if you overfeed your ego, it may lead to something unhealthy."

"Like what, exactly?" Lilly wasn't about to let Ken off the hook because this was precisely where she wanted the discussion to go.

"Well, you could become so full of yourself that you're no longer able to see anyone else as being important or having anything useful to contribute."

"Wow," said Lilly. "So you're saying our egos affect our ability to see the world around us. They color—and possibly distort— our view of people and things. And ideas."

"Well, yeah. We've all known people with overinflated opinions of themselves, and they're a real pain to work with. I mean, look at Jason ..."

Lilly interrupted Ken. "Mmm, let's not bring up people who are not here. What I'd really like to do is throw another question at you because you're on a roll."

"OK, go for it." Ken looked a bit embarrassed at the mild rebuke.

"My question is this: what is it that feeds our self-esteem, especially within a professional setting?"

"That's easy," replied Ken. "Recognition of our abilities."

"I agree, and from the faint head nods I see around the table, I'm clearly not the only one. Let's face it, we all need praise and recognition for our accomplishments. We're programmed from a young age to crave it. As professionals, it often motivates us. But isn't there a way we can balance that desire with other desires like, oh I don't know, how about the desire to see our company do well or the desire to participate in a happy and productive work environment?" Lilly had been looking around the table as she spoke, trying to include everyone in the discussion. When she reached Donna, she found that Donna was staring back.

"I have a question for you," said Donna. "Let's suppose I do have a great idea for improving this happy and productive work environment of ours."

"OK."

"So, why should I share it if I'm not going to get credit for it?"

It seemed that Donna wanted to pick a fight, but Lilly wasn't about to let a question like this derail the discussion, so she fired right back. "What makes you think you won't get credit for it? Haven't you gotten credit in the past for all the remarkable work you've done for the company?"

"What?"

"Everyone knows how amazing you are, Donna, so what's the problem?"

"Well, weren't you just now suggesting we shouldn't be motivated by our desire for recognition?"

"No, not at all. I just don't think we should be consumed by that desire to the exclusion of all else. Also—and I'm really glad you asked the question you did because it reminded me of a related issue—I think we need to distinguish between what goes on outside this room and what goes on when we're consulting together. Outside this room, we need, want, and deserve recognition for our individual achievements, and that's fine as long as it's not taken to ridiculous lengths. Inside this room, however, we need to be able to operate a little differently."

Lilly was still looking at Donna, but before Donna could respond, Kelly cut in.

"What do you mean?"

"What I mean is this, and I'm sort of thinking out loud here: when we meet together, our motivation should be to recognize and embrace the very best ideas and solutions, even if they're not our own, and you know the old saying 'love is blind'? Well, if we're all madly in love with our own ideas and with the thought of being praised for them, we will be blind. In the sense that we won't be able to recognize, much less accept, an even better idea that someone else might have."

"But what if my idea really is the best?" asked Kelly.

"What if it's just plain awful and you only think it's the best?" countered Donna, slightly miffed that Kelly had interfered in her exchange with Lilly.

Lilly headed them both off. "If your idea is bad, then your ability to remove your ego from the equation will make it easier to accept the respectful and well-considered opinions that your peers may express on the subject. And if it's fabulous, we'll all be so detached from our own ego-driven competitiveness that we'll readily recognize its merits. In theory."

"Yeah, in theory." Donna's voice dripped with sarcasm.

Lilly ignored the comment and pressed her point. "Look, people, I'm not saying this is going to be easy. It goes against our nature and upbringing. We live in a very competitive, success-oriented society, and we're all affected by that, myself included. All I'm saying is that we make a commitment, here and now, to try and hold our egos in check when we meet together, and that if we do that, we may discover that the people around us are just as brilliant and insightful as we think *we* are. So what do you say? Can each of us work on subduing our nasty urge to always be right?"

"Yourself included?" said Donna.

"Yes."

"Let me think about it."

"Fine, but I need to know your answer by the end of this meeting." That remark drew some nervous laughs but a scowl from Donna. "What about the rest of you? I see a few headnods, which I will assume means agreement, but some of you still look a little leery, so I'd appreciate hearing your concerns. How about you, Bill?"

The director of marketing had been sitting in stone-faced silence throughout the meeting so far, but now he turned to face Lilly.

"It just doesn't seem right somehow. I mean, it's against everything I believe in. I was always told that in order to succeed I couldn't just rely on dumb luck. I had to make my own breaks, and in order to do that, I might have to step on a few toes or knock a few heads together. That I had to be smarter, tougher, stronger, and bolder than everyone else if I wanted to get ahead. And in my field, I'm also supposed to be more charming than anyone else, at least publicly, but this, I just don't know if I can manage it. It's … it's … heck, I don't know, it's unnatural."

"OK, Bill. I hear you, and I understand it's hard. We've all been fed a steady diet filled with nonsense like 'it's a dog-eat-dog world' or 'you have to look out for number one,' blah, blah, blah. And you know what? I'm sick of it. You know, there were some other lessons we were all given too that we tend to conveniently forget. Things like teamwork and the idea of everybody pulling together when times are tough."

Lilly paused for a few seconds to collect her thoughts and then continued. "Maybe it's the fact that this company is teetering on the brink, but whatever the reason, I've been thinking a lot about how people react during natural disasters. There seem to be two types of people: those who only care about themselves and those who are willing to risk everything to help others. Now that first group of people includes the folks who expect the world to come to an end every three months and are ready to hole up in a cabin filled with provisions while they peer out their windows, shotgun at the ready. And there they are all snug and cozy and paranoid and crazy with the person they love the most in the whole wide world. In fact, the only person or thing they really love is themselves. I don't want to be that person. But Bill, isn't that the group you and I were both trained to be in? How is that attitude any different than that whole do-whatever-it-takes philosophy you were describing?

"Look, I'm not expecting overnight miracles. Changing our mind-set will be a process, and it may take some time, but if you can't accept Rule 6, then you're going to have a really hard time dealing with this next rule because it's a doozy."

Lilly casually picked up her JOGpad, tapped a key, and the JOGboard behind her changed once more. Beneath Rule 6, the following line appeared:

RULE 7: Once you put your idea or opinion out there, it no longer belongs to you.

"OK, people, this is the critical rule that all the others have been leading up to. So before you start shaking your heads, take a moment and reflect on the implications of Rule 7. For example, consider this: some people might say that the consultative approach I have been calling Solution-Building is just brainstorming with some fancy rules of etiquette thrown into the bargain, but is it really? In brainstorming, you might be willing to throw a wild idea out on the table, but it's still your idea and when it gets shot down, you're the one who feels it. But what if instead the ownership of the idea immediately transfers to the group itself? What if no one is allowed to say to you, 'well, your idea won't work because my idea is way better'? What if there is no 'your' and no 'my' at all but simply an evolving group opinion to which you've added—or perhaps even subtracted—a piece? What if criticism simply can't be directed at any individual participant but can only be focused on whatever idea is swirling about in the center of the table? What if you can reach a state where you no longer have to worry about what others may think of your opinion? What if someone that you don't particularly like adds something to the discussion and you can critically and objectively evaluate that contribution without considering who made it?"

"Oh for cryin' out loud! Are you serious? What's next? Are we going to have to start wearing team uniforms and run laps together?"

"Easy there, Donna. You haven't even seen what the uniforms look like yet." Although Lilly's attempt to deflect Donna's anger with humor elicited at least one giggle from the group, Donna was not amused.

"Five minutes ago you were saying, 'Oh, Donna, you're so wonderful! Why wouldn't you get credit for your brilliant ideas?' And now this."

"I was talking specifically about your job performance, Donna. If you recall, I then attempted to draw a distinction between what goes on outside of our meetings and how we conduct ourselves when we are consulting together. These rules only apply to our meetings together. Why is that so difficult to understand? Are these rules so terrible that we can't discuss them calmly and rationally?"

"Lilly, I have a suggestion." It was extremely rare for Brad LaSalle to speak at executive committee meetings, and this immediately got everyone's attention. As legal counsel, he attended these meetings more as a formality and usually only spoke in direct response to legal questions.

"Yes, Brad?"

"I'm wondering if you might consider letting us consult on all of this, without you being present. It would give you an opportunity to go to the cafeteria and get a cup of that nice Darjeeling tea you like so much, and it would give us a chance to see if we can put some of these rules into practice without the specter of coercion hovering in the background. I think fifteen minutes should be sufficient."

The proposal took Lilly completely by surprise. Her first thought was that she was being kicked out of her own meeting, but then she realized that she couldn't very well refuse without losing face. After all, she had been going on and on about how wonderful Solution-Building is, and now she was being asked to allow her staff to do exactly that: consult using that process. The only reasonable response was to smile and accept it.

"I think that's a great idea, Brad." Lilly took a quick look at her watch, got out of her chair, and headed for the door. "See you all in fifteen."

The round-trip to the cafeteria and back took thirteen minutes. That gave Lilly an extra two minutes to kill outside the door to the conference room. She spent it mulling over the same questions she had been asking herself all the way down to the cafeteria and all the way back again. What are they all talking about? What is Brad up to? Are they consulting in good faith, or is this a mutiny? *That doesn't seem likely,* she thought, *especially since they know I'm willing to let people go.* The last two minutes seemed an eternity, but at last Lilly figured that a full fifteen minutes had passed so she opened the door and headed back to her seat.

"Hope I gave you all enough time to consult. So, has the jury reached a verdict, counselor?"

Brad played along with Lilly's half-hearted attempt at legal humor. "We have, your honor. Rules 6 and 7 have been unanimously adopted."

"They have? Really?"

"Yes, but ..."

"But?"

"But, with the proviso that you not ask us here and now to explain how we arrived at this decision. Since this was a Solution-Building–based consultation, our understanding is that the outcome is more important than the details of how we arrived at our decision."

"So you're not going to tell me what your reasoning was?"

"No, but if anyone wishes to speak with you privately after this meeting has ended, there would be no objection."

"Very well, I accept. And since it appears there's nothing more to be said now, this meeting is adjourned. Thank you all very much."

Back at her desk, Lilly couldn't take the suspense any longer. She wanted to know what it was that had caused such a sudden and uncharacteristic change in the group. Brad had said that members of the committee were free to talk about it, but would they? Who would be most likely to talk about it? Mark? Probably, but Lilly was tired of casting Mark in the role of teacher's pet. She wanted to hear it from someone else, so she picked up her phone and dialed a 3-digit extension.

"Kelly Hong here."

"Kelly, this is Lilly. Can you spare me a minute?"

"Sure. What's on your mind?"

"Well, I wanted to know if you could tell me anything about what went on in those fifteen minutes when I was out of the room?"

"Yeah, it's no big deal."

"So? What was it that changed people's minds?"

"Brad simply pointed out that we were looking at the issue all wrong. He said we were all too concerned about getting credit for a good decision. It was more important, in his considered legal opinion, to realize that if a bad decision was made, then none of us could be individually held responsible. We would, in effect, be blameless. Then we all had a good laugh and kept you waiting for fourteen more minutes."

After hanging up the phone, Lilly found herself in a very good mood except that the reactions by Donna and Bill still weighed on her mind. She decided she needed to confront these issues head on, and so she set up separate meetings with each of them in the early afternoon.

Lilly was sitting in her office near the end of the day when Mark entered. "Lilly, I can't help but ask why you met separately with both Donna and Bill, and I wonder what is about to happen."

Lilly began, "I really felt good about the meeting this morning and how most of the team dealt with the Ego Paper. At some point, I would like to know what you thought about it. I just felt that neither one of them was that serious with their responses and commitment during the meeting. I needed to speak with each of them about what their long-term goals and ambitions are with the company. As you and I have discussed, they are both well qualified in their positions, and we can really use them. Fortunately, they both came to the understanding that they would give it a serious shot and participate or they would suffer the same fate as Jason. At this point, I think they will participate in the Solution-Building process we are working with and hopefully the success of JayOGrafix."

"I hope you are right about that, but another thing I wanted to say was that I have been hearing in the hallways that they were called in and fired. People are getting nervous and anxious again, and some of them are jockeying for position."

"For position?"

"To replace Donna and Bill."

"Oh." Lilly sighed. "The more things change the more they stay the same," she said quietly. "What do you think they will be assuming when I talk one-on-one with the rest of the team?"

"Probably that the company is actually going under and everyone will be fired tomorrow," said Mark with a tired smile. "Actually most of them will probably realize that you cannot fire all the managers and will make up something I can't even imagine right now." He paused a second and added, "People love to make negative things up when they don't have information, don't they? So when are you planning to meet with me? Now?"

"You mean we haven't been meeting enough already? Yes, since I plan to meet with everyone else and ask them if they are on board, even those I think are, I am doing the same with you. So, are you willing to do things this way? I am asking for a clear yes or no from everyone."

"Yes," said Mark.

"Thank you. Your support has been very important and valuable to me. I will let you know when I finish with the others so that you can handle any questions coming from the rest of the crew."

After Mark left her office, Lilly asked Pat to set up meetings with the remainder of her staff on Friday morning.

CHAPTER EIGHT

Saturday, a beautiful day for lunch, thought Lilly as she drove to the restaurant to meet Steve and Mara. She really felt she had a handle on these rules so far and was wondering how much longer this would go on. How many more rules can there be? Her staff now seemed to also get what was happening, but she felt she needed to complete this process and really start solving the business issues.

"Good morning," Lilly said as she joined Steve and Mara at their table. They welcomed her and listened while she continued. "This has really been a crazy two weeks in my life, but I think we are getting closer to being on the right track." She told them of the last meeting on Thursday, the introduction of Rules 6 and 7 and how she felt the team was finally coming together.

"It sounds like your Ego Paper idea went over well," Mara said. "I thought that was a great way to introduce Rule 6 and to shock the process."

"Yeah, but I didn't stop to think they would be afraid they were getting their pink slips."

"You also seem pleased but a little hesitant about your introduction of Rule 7," Steve added. "That one seems to be the hardest for most groups and people to accept."

"It looked there was going to be another big fight, but thanks to Brad's timely intervention they consulted and accepted in my absence."

"What?" said Steve.

"Yes, they asked me to leave so they could consult on accepting Rules 6 and 7. So I did, and they agreed." She told them what Kelly had said, and all three had a good laugh.

"That is great. I am so happy for you."

"Okay," Lilly announced, "you said there are more rules, and I am looking forward to them, but how many more are there? How much longer is this going to take? I'm starting to get nervous about spending too much time on this and not getting the company back on its feet."

Mara kindly stepped in. Lilly, there are only two more rules. Steve and I thought we would give them both to you today."

"That's a relief," said Lilly.

"So let's get right to it," said Steve. "They are:

RULE 8: Reaching agreement is more important than being "right."

And,

RULE 9: Once the group has made a decision and moved forward, everyone must support the decision, and you cannot complain if things do not work out.

Steve gave Lilly a page with the two rules printed on it.

"Well," said Lilly, "my first reaction to Rule 8 was a bit strong, but now by reading it I can see how what we have been working on fits into it. We need to all come to agreement on the business issues and then move forward. Rules 6 and 7 flow right into this one, don't they?"

"They do," said Mara.

"You have made terrific progress just getting the senior managers to be willing to try to use Solution-Building. We believe you will be seeing some great results if your team can stick to it," said Steve. "Let's talk about Rule 8. What is the real purpose of your meetings? What are you trying to achieve? You need to all work with each other and make decisions for the betterment of the company, correct?"

"Of course. We can't continue as we have in the past."

"As your team goes through this process and matures, the right decision will show itself through effective consultation," Mara added, "when there is full support from the group and the participants have truly given their ideas to the table."

"I hope we don't have this problem any longer, but I can see how having a person on the team who thinks they need to be right all the time could be quite destructive. There can also be situations that may not be resolved if someone is holding onto their idea because they want credit for it."

"You're correct, and you may only be able to really integrate and appreciate this rule when you see it working," said Mara. "Perhaps the group needs to work on a few less-intense topics, consult, and make a decision. Once that is done, you can point out to everyone the process you just completed, which followed the rules. Hopefully, they will see how successful it is and then choose to embrace it."

"So it is okay to do a process check as we progress?"

"Of course," said Steve, "and you should do it often. That way you can continue to build your skills. Once people let go of their egos, put their ideas out there, see how they don't get trampled, and see how others in the group react and behave, both they and the group continue to improve. In a way, Solution-Building is a self-reinforcing process."

"Before we go on," said Mara, "what is the worst thing that can happen in a meeting where decisions need to be made?"

Lilly thought briefly and realized what Mara was getting at. "Not being able to make a decision. It will paralyze the process and the company, just as it has for months now, but this implies any decision is better than no decision, doesn't it?"

"Not really. Clearly making a decision that is generally considered to be bad is not acceptable; it does mean that you keep going with the goal of getting to agreement. And yes, it may be that there is no workable decision that can be made, but that realization is also a decision of sorts. The true purpose of this Rule 8, based on the previous seven, is to make certain that the group is focused on the goal of any sort of consultation: to reach a decision or a plan of action or whatever else you want to call it. Does this make sense to you?"

"Yes, now it does. I just hope my team agrees."

"Now what do you think of Rule 9?" asked Steve.

"I'm not sure," said Lilly. "What if the decision that was made turns out to be not that good? I mean, what if it doesn't work?"

"Ah," said Steve, "that is always the fun part. Lilly, you will make decisions that may not turn out to be the best at the time, but what that means is that you bring them back to the group, consult on them, and learn. With learning, different, perhaps more effective approaches can be developed and implemented. Part of the value of the rules of Solution-Building is that they encourage objective learning not just about the initial process but also about evaluating results and being willing to change."

"Would you suggest something like an agenda item where we review the decisions made in the previous meetings and make sure they are working?"

"You can, and you probably should for those that aren't working well, but not all. I think that would be quite cumbersome. You should make it clear that if there are problems with a decision, any criticism or discussion with the decision must happen only during your meetings, not in separate discussions outside of the meeting."

Mara jumped in. "What this Rule 9 really means is that once a decision is made, all the members of the group must fully support it, even those who were the most opposed to it during your discussion. It may or may not be the best decision, but it is one the group made, and it must be given a chance to succeed. Those who opposed it may well learn their opposition was unfounded."

"What you cannot have is people undermining the decision after they leave the meeting," added Steve. "If people feel they have the ability to tear down the decision, you are giving them the permission to do just that, or at the least they may do nothing to support it.

"They don't need to leave each meeting like rah-rah cheerleaders, Lilly, but they must not undermine the decisions. The best way to make sure a decision, whether good or bad, workable or unworkable, will fail is to do exactly that. It is no better than what you have now with people actively keeping decisions from being made at all. I know this will take time to get them to change how they behave outside the meetings, but once they see how the process works they will get on board."

"Well, I sure hope this works. My next meeting is Tuesday morning, and I intend to introduce these final two rules then." Lilly looked at her watch. "I should be going now, as I have a lot to work on before my meeting. Thank you again for all you have done for us."

"Lilly," Steve said, "Mara and I have thoroughly enjoyed assisting and accompanying you on this journey. Once this is fully implemented and succeeding, you will look back and say that you can't understand how anything got accomplished before."

Lilly thought about that and admitted she was already thinking that way.

Steve continued, "We should get together again after your next staff meeting and go over what happened. We are both in town for the next month and are at your service."

With that, Lilly got up, hugged each of them, thanked them again and said she would be in touch.

CHAPTER NINE

Tuesday morning Lilly came in even earlier than usual to prepare for the executive meeting and to review how she would start the meeting. The meetings with the individual members on Friday and Monday had gone generally well, but she was still concerned about the full commitment of some of them. She still felt there was resistance. She understood that was mainly because Solution-Building was so different an approach to problem-solving from what people were used to that they were not able to let go of a set of lifelong habits and attitudes, especially on such short notice.

But she felt optimistic. When she first met the time travelers (she smiled as she thought of Steve and Mara in that way) she was reaching the end of her rope with this crew. But now ... she had some hope.

She thought back to something Mara had said just before they parted. "Lilly, you have to have hope, and you have to trust in whatever higher power you believe in. Without hope, without a feeling that there is a solution, you are likely to fail. Henry Ford said, 'If you believe you can do something or if you believe you can't, you're right.' Your team is acting out of fear. The fear of not doing the right thing. That fear is the most powerful paralytic in the universe. All the strife and sniping and resistance is merely a symptom of that fear. Overcoming fear is very difficult for us; our society and its institutions use fear as both a weapon and a tool to, literally, paralyze us into inaction. The major fear that any group of decision-makers has is the fear of making the wrong decision, whatever that may be, with whoever first offers up that decision being blamed. The nine rules we have discussed with you provide one way to mitigate, even eliminate, that fear since we have the key elements of taking ego out and making any and all ideas and decisions group property, allowing them to be rationally and dispassionately evaluated. Your team can do it, if they work by these basic principles, which we have called rules, but that 'can-do' attitude has to start with you. Do you believe in this? Can you make certain all your team knows without doubt that you do? If so, you have a very good chance of seeing JayOGrafix not just survive but also thrive."

Lilly realized that she did believe this would work, that she was not just grasping at any straw that happened to float by. Her conversations with each executive team member made her feel hopeful, even with those from whom she still felt resistance.

Lilly walked into the meeting room a few minutes early to find that she was actually the last person to arrive. Another first! Donna looked at her and said, "Did you sleep here last night? I got in extra early, and your car was already in the lot!"

Smiling, Lilly said, "Looks like a couple of us wanted to be ready this morning." She looked around and said, "Well, since everyone is here, we might as well start early," and, noticing someone had already activated the JOGboard, tapped a key on her JOGpad. The board lit up with one word:

Questions?

"We covered a lot of ground last week, and as each of you knows, I have met individually with all of you. You all know that there are a few more rules to cover today, but first I want to clear out any lingering questions any of you may have about the first seven rules."

A few seconds of silence ensued. Then Brad spoke up.

"I don't have a question but do have a comment. I spent a lot of time over the weekend thinking about the first seven rules, and I think the one that struck me as important is the last one we discussed, number seven, the one that says that when you put an idea forward it is no longer yours but the group's."

"Why is that, Brad?" asked Allison, one of the few times she had spoken up in the meetings. Lilly noted that the question was asked in a neutral and polite tone, something a bit unusual since Allison and Brad did not like each other.

"Well, let's just say you, or perhaps Stan, came up with an idea that ended up being adopted."

"After being dissected and examined from about ten different viewpoints," said Allison. "Then, when its true brilliance is evident, everyone claims it, and I don't get the credit." It was clear to Lilly that this issue was bothering Allison. *Still bothering her*, thought Lilly. That had been one of the points Allison raised when she and Lilly met on Friday.

Brad said, "Perhaps, but what if for some reason such as unexpected changes in technology or the market, it turns out to be a wrong decision? Then who gets the blame? As I see it, and I pointed this out last Thursday, the group gets blamed since the group adopted it. If it had adequate discussion, 'dissection' as you called it, then no one person is held responsible. We will have already examined some other approaches, so we can study why the first one was wrong and take that information into account in looking at alternatives. And not just the previous ideas but also any new ones that arise from the experience with whatever route was chosen." He paused and then added, "As long as we don't bog ourselves down with so many meetings and ideas that nothing happens, that is."

Allison looked a bit skeptical but nodded slowly and said, "I see what you are getting at, and I guess, if we use this approach, we could get a lot of good ideas out for discussion. We have always had plenty of ideas offered up, but afterward the discussions always degenerated into the verbal equivalent of a food fight, and we got nowhere. I would like to think this Solution-Building, with things like parking egos, acting respectful with each other, getting rid of our own agendas, and being able to dump ownership will actually work to get the company back in the groove, and I hope it does. Nothing else has, right?" She looked around the room.

Lilly said, "Brad, Allison, thanks for that. Both of you have made good points. Are there any comments about this from others?"

Jim spoke up. "I want to thank Brad and Allison. They put things into a good perspective. I was also bothered by this issue of putting ideas out and then losing control of them, but I've been thinking since you," he looked at Lilly, "and I met yesterday. I've been unhappy with the way we are wasting time squabbling instead of actually working. I am a production engineer, and in production if a process is not working we change it, scrap it if we need to, and find a way to make our product even if we need a whole new technology. I don't know if this Solution-Building is our new technology for problem-solving and decision-making, but it is past time for results, and I am willing to try. Any potentially workable solution is better than the total inaction we have had since we lost JJ." The room was quiet for a few seconds, and then heads began to nod and a few murmurs of assent were heard.

Lilly said, "Thanks, Jim. I just want to emphasize that I firmly believe this will help us achieve what we need now, which is to set our sights on the future success of the company and work together. Now, at the last meeting, Donna and Bill had the most objections and questions. Do either of you have anything to say after having the last several days to think on it?" She realized she was putting them on the spot but wanted to be sure they, who had expressed the most reservations, were going to be on the same page.

They both began to speak at once, but Bill, in a gesture of courtesy that was a bit of a surprise to her, nodded to Donna to go ahead first. "Well," she said, "I wasn't too happy with this, as you all know, but I do want the company to survive. We have not done a good job of that for months. Quite frankly, I have been thinking of my own position and what would happen if JOG failed. CFOs of failed companies, even companies that fall apart because they cannot adapt to changes, are able to move on. But I don't want to move on from a company I helped succeed in the past just because it's going through a difficult period now. Listening to Brad, Allison, and Jim this morning I realized that I want to be a part of this organization for a long time. I guess that is a long way of saying I want to give this a try." She looked at Lilly and said, "I admit I may need a reminder of the rules now and then. As I suspect all of us may."

"Thanks, Donna," said Lilly, "I appreciate your candor." She looked to Donna's left and said, "Bill? You wanted to say something."

"Yes. I am less convinced than some of the others here. It just cuts against everything I was taught and all my personal experience." He looked at Donna and said, "I gave this a lot of thought and even discussed it—consulted about it?—with my wife this weekend. Unlike CFOs, marketing directors of failed companies have a harder time of moving on. So I also want the company to succeed, even though I haven't been here as long as some of you. I am willing to give it a try."

Before Lilly could say anything, Jim said, "Bill, Donna, you can't just give it a try. You have to fully engage and want to make it work. As I see it, we all have to be willing and able to change the way we think about getting decisions made and how we can optimize the process."

This exchange was interesting, thought Lilly. Bill and Jim had been at odds for months and, it seemed, couldn't agree on anything. Clearly, they must have been thinking about the rules over the last few days. *This*, she thought, *is a good sign*. She said, "Thanks to you, too, for your candor, and I agree with Jim that we need to be fully engaged. Now, Jim said something about a workable solution a few minutes ago. This actually leads us into the next rule." She reached down and the JOGboard displayed:

RULE 8: Reaching agreement is more important than being "right."

She heard a few remarks about what "right" meant, and what if it was wrong. She let the conversation die down before going on.

"We have already discussed what happens when an idea is wrong, so let's examine Rule 8 now. I know, at least for myself, that Rule 7 is tough. I, we all, become invested in our ideas since we take a great deal of pride in doing our job well. We don't try things we consider to be unproductive approaches. I have thought a great deal about Rule 8 and finally realized that just because I think an approach has no value it doesn't mean someone else thinks the same. Perhaps they will have a good reason to consider it valid, and I need to give them a chance to both explain their reasoning and to have the broader group rationally consider it from many different viewpoints. But what if, after all the consultation and 'dissection,' as Allison put it, we have more than one good idea? Or worse, none that appear to be good?"

Allison and Jim both raised their hands, so Lilly just said, "Yes?" The two of them looked at each other and Allison nodded.

"This is one of the places I get a bit concerned with this," said Jim. "It sounds like this turns into an opportunity for endless discussion instead of making any decisions. I can see that this could go on forever, leaving us just where we are now: talking in circles and getting nowhere. Just being polite with each other for a change. How is this group going to reach agreement? We have a long history of not agreeing on anything." He looked at Allison and said, "Were you going to say something similar?" She nodded.

"So," Lilly said, "you are concerned that in the effort to reach agreement we end up talking ourselves to death?"

"Yeah, sort of like Nero fiddling while Rome burned."

Lilly looked around the room, making eye contact with each person. "Is it acceptable to any of you to 'fiddle' while JOG burns? Is the reason that, as Jim said, we have a history of not agreeing? Why do you think we have a history of not agreeing?"

Stan, with a slight smile, said, "Which question do you want to tackle first, Lilly? I'll give you my answer to the first one: No. And I will bet that everyone else here will say the same, or at least I hope so." General agreement appeared in the form of a few statements of "yes" and some headnods.

"Can I give my answer?" asked Bill. When no one objected, he went on. "I first want to say that I am coming, perhaps reluctantly, to the understanding that this Solution-Building can work. And that is largely because, in answer to the question of why we have a history of not agreeing, we have all had our egos out on the table, and they have been controlling our reactions and contributions to the discussions. Of course I have the best ideas, we all say, because I am smart and see the problem more clearly than anyone else. Lilly, I have to admit that when you called me in on Friday I thought you were going to fire me. Afterward, and over the weekend, I thought about just what you said a few minutes ago. Perhaps, even though I am smart, I don't have the entire picture, especially in areas where I don't have the most knowledge, like new technologies we can use, not just in our products but also in our promotional programs. Our egos have obviously gotten in the way, and we have allowed our personal conflicts to lower our estimations of the abilities of each other. Ambition probably enters into it, and if I remember my industrial psych class from college, ambition really blinds us to the contributions of others. I am not sure I understand all the implications of this new rule yet, but it seems to me that it really is about the cumulative application of the previous ones. This is about applying the rules of respect for each other, no personal agendas, playing by the same rules, and taking ego out to actually reach decisions. And if we are serious about any idea becoming group property—something I am still struggling with how to apply—then it makes sense."

Brad spoke then. "Does this 'agreement' have to be unanimous? I am afraid that if it does, we will be fiddling until it's time to lock the doors."

Lilly broke into the conversation. "Great question, Brad, and the answer is no, it does not have to be unanimous. All we need is to have a majority that wants to adopt a specific idea or approach. And this leads us to the ninth and final rule." Lilly touched her pad, and the JOGboard displayed:

RULE 9: Once the group has made a decision and moved forward, everyone must support the decision, and you cannot complain if things do not work out.

The room was once again silent as they took this in. Then, several people started to speak at once.

Lilly jumped in. "Let's take a look at a couple of scenarios. First, we unanimously reach a decision and we implement it. I don't think there would be any disagreement that to get the best results, and from Rule 8, we all need to support the decision and encourage our employees to also support it. Since it is unanimous, that should not be an issue. There will be times when the decision is proven to be correct, which of course we want all the time, and we will all witness the success. There will also be times when the decision is proven not to be correct. When that happens, we will revisit the decision in a subsequent meeting and modify or change it. We may just realize it was bad and need to throw it out completely and find another."

"But what about the other possibility: that we are not unanimous, that there are some who do not think it is the better way to deal with whatever the issue may be? What if they do not support it and by whatever means let their employees know they do not? What happens then?"

Before she could go on, Ken spoke. "They will not encourage their people to try to make it work, I suppose, which, of course, raises the probability that it won't. Isn't that part of human nature? That if we don't believe in something we are less likely to give it our all?"

Allison said, "And if our boss doesn't like it, wouldn't we feel it was in our best interest not to either?" She looked around and added, "At least with some bosses."

Lilly decided this was not a direction she wanted the discussion to go, so she said, "The important thing here is that when we have people who do not support a decision or, worse, actively oppose it, the result is, as Ken said, that it will be more difficult to actually find out if the result is positive. And without positive results this company is not going to survive, is it?"

Bill spoke next. "I am having a problem with this one too. All my life, I was taught that I had to be a mover, a shaker, and be better to get ahead, and that getting ahead was the all-important thing in a career. What if someone's opposition turns out to be correct? Wouldn't they be right to continue it?"

Donna said, "As I see it, you can't know something won't work until you give it a serious try. Otherwise, failure becomes a self-fulfilling prophecy. I am beginning to understand something else here, and that is either we can work together and all of us support the company, and I guess each other, or we can continue to do what we have been doing and watch the company fall apart. Besides, Bill, do you think that if the company fails because we cannot make the necessary decisions any of us will be seen as 'movers and shakers'? I doubt it."

Lilly decided it was time to make something clear. "It's important to understand that decisions are made by the team, not by individuals on the team. Looking back on all the rules we have discussed," she touched her JOGpad, and all nine rules appeared on the JOGboard behind her, "would you agree that when we follow this approach, when we are consulting as equals, that our decisions will be better and more likely to have a chance at successful outcomes?"

She looked around the room. Most of the participants appeared to be thinking, she hoped about what she had just said. There were a few nods and a couple of quiet assents. Finally, Jim spoke.

"Maybe I am just being an anal engineer, but I want to get on with our work. I am perfectly happy to do whatever it takes to help the company. This sounds good in the abstract, but we need to agree to one other thing first before we decide to do this: that we are all going to follow these rules and be willing to be reminded of that when we fall off the wagon, so to speak. In other words, follow Rule 1 and play by the same rules. These." And he pointed at the JOGboard.

Kelly spoke for the first time in the meeting. "I agree, and I plan to introduce these to my department when we meet later today. If they have any chance of working here, they will also work for us."

The looks of surprise on the faces of several others indicated that they had not thought to take this Solution-Building process any further than the executive committee. Stan said, "I hadn't really thought about that, but you are right. I think I will too."

Mark said, "To be honest, I am seeing more agreement at this table than we ever had under JJ, but let me ask a question. We have heard from Jim, Kelly, and now Stan, all of whom seem to be on board. What about the rest of you? This won't work unless all of us are agreed to make it work. For the record, I'm in and ready."

"What about it?" asked Lilly, "I want to hear it from each of you. In or out? And for the record, I am in too."

"And if we are not 'in'?" asked Brad.

"What do you think?"

"That 'out' may mean we are out the door."

Lilly remained silent and simply looked at each one in turn. Each, including Brad, said, "In."

It seemed to Lilly that the group heaved a collective sigh when the last person responded. Then Ken spoke up.

"Well, why don't we get started, then? What are we going to do about this new product from Haze?" He looked at Kelly. "Do you or your team have any details on what they are doing yet?"

They got to work.

CHAPTER 10—EPILOGUE

I don't see why we are spending time on this technology again. It hasn't worked!" said Ken, for the third or fourth time in the meeting, sounding slightly exasperated.

"But do we know why? If we knew that, we may be able to use the information and find a way to make it work," said Lilly. She was looking at Kelly.

"I don't know why it doesn't work, Lilly, nor does my staff. Perhaps the approach should be to go back to the basic research team and forget about getting this to market in the near term. Maybe it will never work. We did discuss several ideas that we felt would work, but we decided to try to leapfrog everything and put a whole new technology in place. That may have to wait. It may even have been a big mistake, but we believe we can still come up with most of the improvements we wanted, just not as scientifically elegant."

"Let's talk about that," said Bill. "Most of our customers aren't even aware of what scientific elegance, as Kelly calls it, is. They want a product that meets and preferably exceeds their expectations and needs. Would you agree, Allison?"

"Yes." She paused and then added, "The Haze Systems' product had a lot of hype about elegance and advanced science, but in the end did not perform nearly as well as they promised, and we have yet to hear that they are able to solve some of the glitches that arose. The market isn't pleased with them, and our sales staff has been told that customers are now looking to us to deliver something that at least does what Haze said theirs would do."

The discussion went on, and ideas were put out on the table. In the end, one of the ideas that had been sidelined at a meeting several months ago was brought forward, and a decision was made to go with what they could do now and spend time in the R&D group examining the "failed" technology to determine if there was something they missed. The decision was unanimous, as many were now becoming. It was also made without serious contention or argument, which is not to say that it was easy or that members of the team were not willing to state their positions strongly, but now these strong positions were backed up by logic, data, and perhaps above all else, courtesy. The execs had learned over the past few months to listen to each other's questions and comments with enough objectivity that they were able to see both strengths and weaknesses in their own ideas and those of the others and were feeling more comfortable with Solution-Building.

When the meeting ended and everyone got back to work, Lilly sat in the conference room for a while thinking back on the past months. They had made some good decisions and some that did not work out, but they had been able to avoid several that had, on the surface, looked good but on deeper analysis had many flaws. They had gradually come to trust one another and were able to work together. The result was that when it became obvious that a decision was not going to produce the desired endpoint, they were able to make changes without recriminations or blaming. Fortunately, thanks to Solution-Building, there had not been many of those. The biggest disappointment came today. They had tried to implement an advanced nanotechnology into the product line that, had it worked, would have made possible the greatest advancement in detailed real-time 3-D engineering design on the market. Now they would have to look at something that would likely be an incremental advance instead. R&D, engineering, and production actually believed the nanotech approach would work and were already planning a priority program to work out the bugs that had plagued them for months. Lilly smiled as she thought of the three execs forming a development team that included both marketing and sales for perspective on the market and customers. The team planned to use Solution-Building as the basis for moving the program forward. She was especially happy that the program working team did not include just the execs themselves; they were bringing their top people for sure but were allowing other ideas to be considered.

We are not out of the woods yet. Haze rushed out its product with bugs that were bigger than anyone anticipated, and therefore JOG still had a window in which to compete and, once again, a team that was willing to work together to do it. Her confidence that JOG would thrive had been growing week by week, and her team was telling her they felt the same way.

Lilly maintained her contact with Steve and Mara. She kept them informed, in general, of the progress of the company, but their relationship was more social than professional. Steve and Mara were impressed with the fact that the Solution-Building approach seemed to be working well, and when asked if they would be interested in a more formal relationship, they demurred, saying that the JOG staff appeared to have taken to the process so well that no further accompaniment along that path was needed. It now needed to be the team's process—not an outsider's.

The drop in sales had stabilized, and it appeared that the market was waiting. JOG, with a truly better way of doing things, intended to deliver. *Would deliver*, Lilly added to herself, as she got up and headed back to her office.

ABOUT THE AUTHORS

Kevin Smith, a Colorado native, has been fortunate to work with and for companies of all sizes, from small start-ups to Fortune 500 corporations. During his youth, Kevin was involved in many organizations such as 4-H, where he always seemed to seek out leadership roles and, at an early age saw a need for consensus building. In the various organizations and companies that followed, he served on many committees and teams. After being introduced to the Bahá'í faith by his wife, Juli, he learned about consultation as an effective method in decision-making. Kevin decided to find a mechanism to share this method and as such sought the help of Michael and Gordon to write this book. Kevin and Juli live in Colorado, have two children and three granddaughters.

Michael Burke has worked in organizations from start-ups with as few as three employees to multinational corporations and has started a number of companies in his career. He has been a director of departments and divisions and served on the boards of directors of non-profits, schools, and small companies and has always sought workable solutions to issues. His involvement in many projects requiring critical decision-making including international pharmaceutical product development and planning significant strategic expansions taught him that the current approaches to making those decisions are flawed. Since being introduced to the Bahá'í Faith by his wife, Susan, he has been studying and practicing the consultative approach to decisions in all situations. When Kevin approached him about writing this book he enthusiastically agreed. Michael and Susan live in Colorado and have two daughters, one living in Europe. Michael teaches medical subjects at a private college in Denver and uses the approaches in this book as much as possible in that work.

Gordon McComb has been actively involved for thirty years in all phases of the software development industry, designing, developing and managing the production of complex financial systems, primarily for agencies in the public sector. He lived a number of years in Europe in his youth and met his wife, Lauren, while attending college in Germany. The experience of being immersed in different cultures nurtured his love for language and writing and has given him an appreciation for diverse world views. Raised a Baha'i, he has served for many years on its elected consultative bodies and has seen the stark contrast between the decision-making process in the Baha'i Faith and that which is used by public sector organizations. Gordon and Lauren currently reside in Colorado and have three grown children.

The three authors have each been married for over 30 years and have utilized consultation throughout their lives. Their desire is to get this process integrated at many levels, as it is a much more effective method to build solutions.

APPENDIX A—GUIDING PRINCIPLES

True enlightenment through consultation cannot be achieved unless everyone understands and agrees to "the Rules" of **Solution-Building.**

RULE 1: Everyone plays by the same rules.

Principle: Unless everyone abides by the same principles of consultation, you cannot have effective consultation.

Ground rules are governing structures required for any group activity to be effective. Without such rules, the result will be chaos. Consider what would happen if, to play baseball, seven players showed up with gloves, bats, and balls, one with a basketball, and another with a tennis racket. This applies to the business setting as well since the employees and managers must function as essentially a coordinated organism to succeed. In the case of a for-profit business, success is measured by financial parameters, while for a nonprofit organization, success is measured by the efficient use of resources to deliver the goods and services they provide to the largest number of possible recipients.

The subsequent Guiding Principles assume this first rule is endorsed and applied by all involved in the consultative decision-making process.

RULE 2: You must come to the group ready and willing to participate.

Principle: Be an active participant. Withholding your opinion could inhibit reaching the best decision.

Everyone has ideas, thoughts, and opinions on a wide range of topics, including issues facing the business or other organization in which they work or serve. Passively sitting in a meeting and not offering any ideas is like a member of a sports team walking up and down the playing area ignoring his teammates and not participating, effectively making the team one player short. Everyone must consider themselves capable of offering worthwhile contributions, even if they truly believe they have nothing to offer. Their viewpoint is unique because of background, training, and experience. By not speaking up, they may deprive the group of a valuable perspective or insight that could help it reach their goal much more effectively.

Of course, an individual may feel intimidated by others in the group and feel that he may face criticism for or attacks of the ideas offered. This leads us directly to:

RULE 3: Treat everyone in the group with courtesy and respect.

Principle: Respect and value everyone else's opinion. On this issue, they may be the most informed.

Discourtesy to and disrespect for others is unfortunately all too commonplace. A harsh word or phrase often will spark the same in return, and in short order the behavior either escalates or results in one party withdrawing, thus depriving the discussions of possibly valid and useful inputs. See number 2 above. While disagreements will occur, they need not be accompanied by rancor or other reactions that tend to belittle ideas or the individuals who offer them to the group, irrespective of the actual value of those ideas.

For some, courtesy and respect may be interpreted as a sign of weakness, but the truth is actually the opposite. Indeed, when one shows these two traits, they are a sign of strength, confidence, and personal balance. As a result, they are often returned. The person considering using the Solution-Building approach to decisions is more likely to seriously examine the strengths of ideas put forth by others in a positive atmosphere of respect and courtesy rather than in a negative setting. When members of a team dismiss ideas or suggestions from others, they deprive the team of potentially valuable contributions.

RULE 4: Act as though the person whose respect is most important to you is watching how you behave.

Principle: Call yourself to the very highest standard of behavior whenever you consult with others.

As a child, your parents might have told you to "be on your best behavior" when meeting certain people. As an adult, your behavior is likely to vary widely depending on who you are with and where you are. You can probably come up with situations, either real or imagined, where you would want to be on your best behavior. Meeting a personal hero of yours, being interviewed for your dream job, or speaking to your child's class at school about what you do for a living are examples that might come to mind. Now imagine which person or persons you would least like to disappoint in those situations. If they were to attend your next meeting as silent witnesses, would they approve or disapprove of how you acted and spoke?

RULE 5: No personal agendas allowed.

Principle: The purpose of Solution-Building is not to advance your own personal interests.

The goal of group consultation is to find the best solution to a problem or to determine the truth about a particular issue. You are not there to impress others or try to get people to like you or curry favor or seek to benefit personally. If your motivation is self-serving, then you will have great difficulty fairly evaluating any opinions put forth that advance goals at variance with your own purposes. This internal conflict of interest will undermine the consultative process of Solution-Building. Furthermore, if other members of the group perceive that you are self-serving, they will not give credence to anything you have to contribute.

RULE 6: Park your ego at the door or you don't get a seat at the table.

Principle: It's more important for the group to succeed than it is for you to be successful.

That insistent sense of self-importance, that innate belief that your opinions are "correct" is very difficult to overcome. It is a major barrier to successful and meaningful discussion because it prevents you from dispassionately listening to the views of others in the group. It causes you to believe that if someone else is right, then you must be wrong, and that's something that the ego won't permit. It drives you to hold on to your own opinions, even in the face of compelling evidence to the contrary.

Solution-Building, however, is not some sort of zero-sum game of winning opinions balancing out losing opinions. Indeed, the very notion of "my opinion" versus "your opinion," which is so vigorously promoted in many cultures and societies, has no particular meaning in this form of group consultation. Those individual views are simply small components of a larger group opinion.

RULE 7: Once you put your idea and/or opinion out there, it no longer belongs to you.

Principle: Don't fall in love with or be attached to your opinion.

As we saw with the previous rules, our egos, feelings, and need for recognition need to be checked. If we are putting out ideas only because we want to get credit, then we are in the wrong place. The entire team and organization will succeed when members can divorce themselves from their ideas. Letting go of your opinion once is has been voiced allows for easier discussion and changes.

If a member of the team starts to criticize when suggestions or ideas are introduced, then that idea is killed, and the person who submitted it feels insulted. Only when the team matures to the point that members can freely submit ideas and discuss them openly can they then move on with success.

RULE 8: Reaching agreement is more important than being "right."

Principle: The purpose of the group is to consult and reach agreement on various decisions.

Reaching agreement is for the betterment of the company or organization, not for the personal betterment of the individuals. As discussed in Rule 7, an idea from an individual member is only a suggestion at the time until full consultation. The point of consultation is to reach a decision, not for an individual to be "right." With effective Solution-Building, the right decision will show itself when there is full support from the group.

The issue we struggle with is that we all want to get credit for an idea, especially when it succeeds. Solution-Building does not take this away, but the main goal is to reach agreement. Individuals who only make suggestions with the intent of receiving praise will not succeed in this process.

RULE 9: Once the group has made a decision and moved forward, everyone must support the decision, and you cannot complain if things do not work out.

Principle: You may not criticize any decision to which you were a party. You must support and carry out the decision wholeheartedly.

Once the team makes a decision, everyone must support it, or it will fail. The implementation of the decision will occur in the workplace. Only if everyone supports the process will that decision be given the chance to show if it was the correct one. From time to time, we may not fully agree with the decision, but we must support it and give it the proper chance to succeed. If it succeeds, then great! If not, then it is time to refine the decision. During the implementation process, other information may come to light that shows the decision was not the best and can be improved. The team will need to discuss and consult again and make a new and improved decision.